I Have a Dream: A Report Card Fifty Years after Dr. King's Assassination

Alvin A. Plexico, Ph.D.

ISBN: 1975681924
ISBN-13: 9781975681920

Contents

Introduction

On June 19, 2017, I took my youngest daughter, Savannah, to the Clayborn Temple in Memphis, Tennessee, to see the PRIZM Chamber Orchestra's "Juneteenth" concert, "Seven Last Words of the Unarmed." Some may know that this was the location where Dr. Martin Luther King Jr. met with nearly fifteen thousand marchers on March 28, 1968, as part of the sanitation workers' strike.

While at the concert, I was reminded that the fiftieth anniversary of Dr. King's assassination was less than a year away, and I wondered what plans there might be to commemorate this in my current hometown of Memphis, where Dr. King was killed and where the National Civil Rights Museum is located.

A week later, I was showing Dr. King's "I Have a Dream" speech as part of a public speaking course I teach for a university located at Naval Support Activity Mid-South in Millington, Tennessee. During the speech, it occurred to me that we all have a responsibility to remember the sacrifice that Dr. King paid. It wasn't enough to wonder what someone else was going to do. The real question should be, what was I going to do?

Later that night, I woke up with the idea of writing a book that reviewed the progress made since Dr. King's speech, while acknowledging the tremendous amount of progress that still needs to be made.

Thus, *I Have a Dream: A Report Card Fifty Years after Dr. King's Assassination* began.

Over the course of this year, I've researched, written, edited, edited some more, edited even more, and asked others to review this work in hopes that we can gain an appreciation of how far we've come, while making an honest assessment of how far we still need to go.

I would not feel right earning any money from this project, so all proceeds from the sale of this book will be donated to the National Civil Rights Museum.

Please post your comments and questions at www.IHaveADreamReportCard.com.

Grades

I consider these definitions as a starting point for conversation. I don't pretend to be an expert in any of these issues from a policy viewpoint, let alone a personal viewpoint. I welcome others to disagree with my assessment of each issue, as well as those who wish to offer other descriptions for each grade.

A = true today
B = mostly true today
C = progress made, but work remains
D = lack of sufficient progress made
F = little to no progress made

These dreams represent my modern-day interpretation of key excerpts from Dr. King's "I Have a Dream" speech, originally delivered on August 28, 1963. Others may draw their own conclusions from the speech, and I welcome those who have a different interpretation of how Dr. King's dreams can be applied to civil rights issues today.

Grade	Dream
C	Content of Character (White Privilege)
C–	Democracy (Disenfranchisement)
C–	Economic Opportunity (Economic Reality)
B+	Equal Access (Public Accommodation)
D	Faith (Church Diversity)
F	Justice (Racial and Criminal)
A–	Marriage Equality (Interracial)
B–	Peaceful Protest (First Amendment)
C	Police Brutality (Black Lives Matter)
D	Urgency of Now
C	Voting Rights (Gerrymandering)

Urgency of Now

We have also come to this hallowed spot to remind America of the fierce urgency of now. This is no time to engage in the luxury of cooling off or to take the tranquilizing drug of gradualism.

As we walk, we must make the pledge that we shall always march ahead. We cannot turn back. There are those who are asking the devotees of civil rights, 'When will you be satisfied?'...We are not satisfied, and we will not be satisfied until justice rolls down like waters and righteousness like a mighty stream.

It's just as true today as it was when Dr. King spoke these words in 1963. There are real people, real families, real communities suffering because of the apathy of many of our fellow citizens and the inability of people in power to make real change.

I'm not sure this is an actual dream that requires a grade, but if it does, I would rate it as a D. I'm guilty of going about my normal day focused on my family, my work, my life, my…my…my…me…me…me. I never think about taking proactive steps to help those in need, especially my neighbors of color.

A few years ago, we took the opportunity of an empty nest to change churches. When we looked for a new church home, we had two criteria. First, we wanted a church that reflected the great diversity we're blessed with here in the Memphis area. Second, we wanted a church that spent more time reaching out to those in need than it did judging those who may have different beliefs. Fortunately, we found where we believe the Lord wants us to serve at the Life Church.

Each week, members of the Life Church, through the Memphis Dream Center, provide thousands of meals to children in need and through the Youth Leadership Network provide after-school literacy and leadership programs that resulted in 100 percent of students increasing at least one letter grade in each subject and advances in reading levels.[1]

While my wife and I play a small role in supporting the work of the Life Church and the Memphis Dream Center, I know that if I'm honest with myself, there's a lot more I could be doing to meet Dr. King's call of "the urgency of now."

Another relevant quote from Dr. King is from his 1965 commencement address at Oberlin College:

> Let nobody give you the impression that the problem of racial injustice will work itself out. Let nobody give you the impression that only time will solve the problem. That is a myth, and it is a myth because time is neutral. It can be used either constructively or destructively. And I'm absolutely convinced that the people of ill will in our nation—the extreme rightists—the forces committed to negative ends—have used time much more effectively than the people of good will. It may well be that we will have to repent in this generation, not merely for the vitriolic works and violent actions of

the bad people who bomb a church in Birmingham, Alabama, or shoot down a civil rights worker in Selma, but for the appalling silence and indifference of the good people who sit around and say, "Wait on time." Somewhere we must come to see that human progress never rolls in on wheels of inevitability. It comes through the tireless efforts and the persistent work of dedicated individuals. Without this hard work, time becomes an ally of the primitive forces of social stagnation. So we must help time and realize that the time is always right to do right.[2]

I encourage you to make the time to do what is right. Get involved with a local or national organization dedicated to equality. I mention several throughout this book, and I encourage you to share even more by posting a comment at www.IHaveADreamReportCard.com.

Content of Character (White Privilege)

I have a dream that my four little children will one day live in a nation where they will not be judged by the color of their skin but by the content of their character.

I grade this dream a C. When we don't know the content of someone's character, we often make assumptions about his or her character based on the color of his or her skin.

Overt racism may be rare today, but racism, along with its cousin, implicit bias, still exists, and its effects are still potent.

According to *New York Times* columnist Nicholas Kristof, "The greatest problem is not with flat-out white racists, but rather with the far larger number of Americans who believe intellectually in racial equality but are quietly oblivious to injustice around them. Too many whites unquestioningly accept a system that disproportionately punishes blacks…We are not racists, but we accept a system that acts in racist ways."[3]

Unfortunately, there are still many people who hold and even share racist views. Just look at some of the rants available on social media. It's disgusting. It's a horrible example for future generations. It's a sad reflection of many hearts that feel free to lash out behind a curtain of anonymity.

One example my wife shared with me was in a college course about multicultural counseling at the University of Memphis. A lady shared a story about one of her neighbors who had recently moved because every time his sons would take advantage of the community pool paid for by the homeowner's association, local police would be called because "there were kids trespassing on private property." This neighbor, who happened to be African American, was the president of the homeowner's association at the time, but his neighbors assumed that because his sons were black, they were not residents of the neighborhood.

Another example I learned from my son-in-law, who grew up in a small Texas town and graduated from high school in 2013. He shared that "it was pretty much my skin color first, and then they found out how I acted and spoke. They would say something like, 'You speak well.' And I would say something like, 'Well, this is how I normally talk.'"[4] The point was that people he met seemed surprised by the way he talked or acted based on how they had already prejudged him by the color of his skin.

He also shared an experience he had during picture days at school. "I'm sitting in a chair and this teacher comes up and instead of saying, 'You in that shirt,' she said, 'Hey, little black boy.' Everybody got silent, and I was shocked because no one said anything. I got singled out as that 'little black boy.'"[5]

Unfortunately, "little black boy" was not the worst thing he was called. "A couple of high schoolers helped out refereeing little league basketball games. Of course, nobody likes the referee because you're calling [penalties] against their kids. I remember walking into the parking lot after a game, and someone in a truck slowed down and called me the n-word and told me how terrible a ref I was.

I knew that being in that town, you can't say anything, and you can't really do anything. You have to sit there and accept it and go on."[6]

As I listened to my son-in-law describe this experience from just a few years ago, I wondered how many other people of color had to "accept it and go on"? How many times does this happen today? How long can we expect people to "accept it and go on" before we all decide that enough is enough? Something must be done, even if that something is how we respond to others who share overt or covert racist ideas.

Sometimes, I meet people who assume that they can openly share their racist feelings because these people and I both happen to lack pigment in our skin. For example, I was having new tires installed at a local store when another man with whom I was sitting remarked that there were more and more Mexicans working in the area. He said that at least they had a good work ethic as opposed to the blacks down in Memphis. After I paused for a moment to make sure I heard him correctly, I replied that I did not share his opinion because for one thing, my current boss (a two-star navy admiral) was one of the hardest-working men I knew. He said something like, "Is that right?" I replied, "Yes," and then moved to another section in the waiting area. This was 2012, so not that long ago.

This interaction bothered me for a long time—not just that it happened but that I feel like I could have said more or done something different. It still haunts me to this day, when I reflect on how little progress we've made in this area at the individual level. It bothers me more when I realize that I don't know what to do about it. I naïvely thought that time would eventually get rid of all racists, but that's not the case. Many of those who engage in racist behavior today are young people. Something needs to be done. I only wish I knew what that something was because it's not just individuals who harbor racism in their heart; racism is ingrained in our society.

Jim Wallis notes that racism includes "the power to dominate and enforce oppression, and that power in America is mostly still in white hands…Much of American racism as it is experienced today is rooted in the broader structures of society such as education, employment, housing, and the criminal justice system."[7]

He goes on to describe racism as "prejudice plus power—the power that, by and large, white people have and people of color don't—and racism is rooted in the identity of whiteness. And recent research shows that those implicit biases exist in most all people—white, but also black and other people of color."[8]

The good news is that the implicit biases we all have can be changed, but it takes time, and more importantly, it requires an awareness of the bias(es) and a deliberate desire and focus on changing them.[9]

The challenge is that many of us are not even aware of our bias(es). In fact, many of my white friends will become very defensive if someone implies that they're biased, much less prejudiced or racist. Denying our own implicit bias(es) will not change the truth, which is that there are still realities of racism in our society today—realities that hurt people of color and deny all of us (whites as well as people of color) the full benefits of a diverse society and community.

Enjoying the benefits of diversity is not an experience most enjoy because "de facto economic and housing segregation still exists for the majority of African Americans, and the geography of race still separates most black Americans from most white Americans. Public Religion Research Institute's 2013 American Values Survey found that the social networks of white Americans are an astonishing 91 percent white, with fully 75 percent of whites having entirely white social networks."[10]

Many of my white friends will become defensive about accusations of implicit bias, and they'll become downright apoplectic when confronted with a term such as *white privilege*.

When discussing white privilege, I try to avoid making people feel ashamed or guilty. I'll often hear replies such as, "My ancestors never owned slaves," or "I grew up very poor," or "I worked hard for everything I have." Each of these may be true, but they don't negate the truth that in our society, whites enjoy the benefit of the doubt based on the color of their skin, rather than the content of their character (good or bad).

A personal example may help refine this point. In the thirty-plus years I've driven a car, I've been stopped maybe a dozen times or so. I've received a ticket twice, both for speeding, which means that every other time I received a warning (for which I am grateful). I assumed this was the norm until I was talking with a fellow naval officer, who happened to be African American. He informed me that he had been pulled over countless times and almost always received a ticket if he had been speeding or allowed to proceed without a ticket (after a thorough search of his vehicle), if he was pulled over without having been speeding. I asked what he meant by a thorough search of his vehicle, and he stated that every time he's pulled over by a police officer, he's asked to get out of the car so his vehicle can be searched. I have NEVER been asked to get out of my car by a police officer. Never. Not once in all the years I have been driving, and yet, my friend has been asked to get out of his vehicle by a police officer so many times that this is considered normal. Our sense of a normal traffic stop is different because of the white privilege I'm afforded by both white officers as well as officers of color.

Another example that saddens me to this day happened a few years ago when I was eating with a neighbor friend of mine at a fast-food restaurant along a highway. As I looked outside, I noticed that a middle-aged African American lady had been pulled over by a police officer. She was standing at the back of her car in the cold, misty morning while the officer checked the inside of her vehicle. I asked my neighbor why he thought this was so, and without hesitating he said, "Because she's black." I asked him if he thought this was right, and he thought for a moment and then replied, "Probably not," after which he went right back to eating. The point is that it didn't affect him, so it wasn't his concern. But shouldn't it be? Shouldn't we all be concerned if some in our society are treated differently based on the color of their skin?

Another personal example of white privilege happened when my wife and I were shopping for a briefcase at a local office supply store. After paying for the briefcase, the theft alarm went off as I exited the store. The young lady at the register, who happened to be African American, waved me along assuring me it was OK to continue. As I walked to my car, it occurred to me that she never checked the inside of the briefcase. I could have walked out with just about anything from the store. I wonder if she assumed that a middle-aged white guy wouldn't steal. But would she have given the same benefit of the doubt to an African American male? I'll never know for sure, but it reminded me that the color of my skin affords me benefits, the benefits of white privilege, that I rarely even notice.

Again, it's not about feeling guilty or ashamed. I can't change the color of my skin. As Jim Wallis reminds us, it's "Not to make white people feel guilty and defensive about the past but to free all of us to take responsibility for a new and better future—especially for our children."[11]

"A first step for white people, I think, is to not be afraid to admit that we have benefited from white privilege. It doesn't mean we are frauds who have no claim to our success. It means we face a choice about what we do with our success."[12]

Another response I often hear from some is that they're color-blind to race or that we should live in a society where color doesn't matter. "But color does matter. We are not supposed to be colorblind, because there are colors and shades and complexities within the shades, so we should see the colors, and injustices, and oppressions, and exploitation clearly and work for liberation…"[13]

Some do not want to see color because it makes them feel uncomfortable. Others see color and feel uncomfortable because of the changing demographics in our society. Like it or not, change is coming. According to Pew Research Center population projections, whites will make up less than half of the US population by 2050.[14]

As our society changes, will we have more opportunities to interact with others who look, think, and act differently? Will this interaction lead to a better understanding and appreciation for our differences? If so, perhaps we can move closer to achieving Dr. King's dream of judging others "not by the color of their skin but by the content of their character."[15]

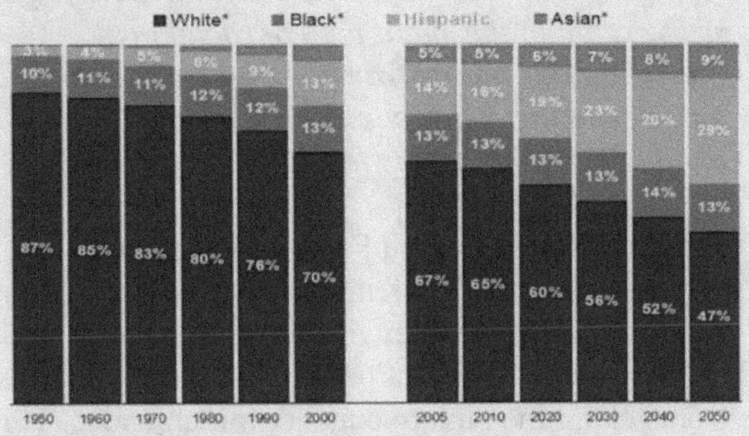

The Changing Face of America,1950-2050
Percent of Total Population
White*
Black*
Hispanic
Asian*
1950
1960
1970
1980
1990
2000
2005
2010
2020
2030
2040
2050
3%
4%
5%
6%
9%
10%
11%
11%
12%
13%
12%
13%
87%
85%
83%
80%
76%
70%
5%
5%
6%
7%
8%
9%
14%
16%
19%
23%
26%
29%
13%
13%
13%
13%
14%
13%
67%
65%
60%
56%
52%
47%
Source: Pew Research Center Population Projections.

Justice (Racial and Criminal)

Now is the time to rise from the dark and desolate valley of segregation to the sunlit path of racial justice. Now is the time to lift our nation from the quicksands of racial injustice to the solid rock of brotherhood. Now is the time to make justice a reality for all of God's children.

I grade this dream as an F. As a nation, we have a long way to go to meet Dr. King's dream of rising from "the dark and desolate valley of segregation to the sunlit path of racial justice." In fact, I believe we've regressed on many fronts along the path to equal criminal justice. This is why it's one of the rare areas in which I offer a failing grade.

Jim Wallis offers this assessment: "As a result of our profoundly unequal law enforcement system, we have seen much of the progress of the civil rights movement stalled, and in many cases rolled back, in a number of insidious ways…The treatment of black men by police and a still-racialized criminal justice system in America became a painful and controversial national issue over the last few years, making visible what has been true for decades…We are the nation with the highest rate of incarceration in the world, a phenomenon that is inexorably linked to our history of racial inequality…Only in a country where we have learned to tolerate evidence of racial injustice would this be seen as something other than a national crisis."[16]

Consider this data to support Wallis's assessment that "statistics on mass incarceration and our criminal justice system reveal a startling racial disparity":[17]

The United States contains 5 percent of the world's population and 25 percent of the world's prisoners.[18]

African Americans make up 40 percent of the incarcerated population, despite making up only 13 percent of the population.[19]

One out of every fifteen African American men and one in thirty-six Latino men in the United States are currently incarcerated. Meanwhile, only 1 in every 106 white men is behind bars.[20]

One in three African American men will be imprisoned at some point in his lifetime. This compares to one in six Latino men and one in seventeen white men.[21]

African Americans are about three times more likely to be arrested than are whites.[22]

African Americans comprise 14 percent of regular drug users but comprise 37 percent of those arrested for drug offenses.[23]

From 1980 to 2007, about one in three of the 25.4 million adults arrested for drugs was African American.[24]

More than 60 percent of the people in prison today are people of color.[25]

In 2003, black men were nearly twelve times more likely to be sent to prison for a drug offense than white men. Yet national household surveys show that whites and African Americans use and sell drugs at roughly the same rates.

Some may look at the above data and conclude that there's been an increase in crime over the past few decades, but this is not the case. "This increase is not due to rising crime rates but rather was caused mainly by changes in sentencing law and policy."[26]

The injustice doesn't end when the person has paid his or her debt to society because "those convicted of felonies—even if the felony in question was a nonviolent offense such as possession of an illegal drug—find themselves stripped of many of the rights that most American citizens take for granted."[27]

"The tragic irony here is that many of the rights they forfeit are precisely those that people of color fought for during the civil rights movement, such as 'the right to vote, the right to serve on juries, and the right to be free from legal discrimination in employment, housing, and access to education and public benefits.'"[28]

It may be easy for those not affected by the criminal justice system to ignore or make excuses for the racial disparity in our nation. However, President Barack Obama offered this germane advice: "When any part of the American family does not feel like it is being treated fairly, that's a problem for all of us. It's not just a problem for some. It's not just a problem for a particular community or a particular demographic. It means that we are not as strong as a country as we can be. And when applied to the criminal justice system, it means we're not as effective in fighting crime as we could be."[29]

This, like many issues regarding race, is complicated because there are many root causes along with many opportunities to make a difference. This advice from Wallis offers a path for consideration: "If we are serious about solving this problem, then we're going to not only have to help the police, we're going to think about what can we do, the rest of us, to make sure that we're providing early education to these kids, to make sure that we're reforming our criminal justice system so it's not just a pipeline from schools to prisons, so that we're not rendering men in these communities unemployable because of a felony record for a non-violent drug offense, that we're making investments so that they can get the training they need to find jobs."[30]

The folks at the Sentencing Project offer the following as a place to start:[31]

> Eliminating mandatory minimum sentence and cutting back on excessively lengthy sentences; for example, by imposing a twenty-year maximum on prison terms.
>
> Shifting resources to community-based prevention and treatment for substance abuse.
>
> Investing in interventions that promote strong youth development and respond to delinquency in age-appropriate and evidence-based ways.

Examining and addressing the policies and practices,
conscious or not, that contribute to racial inequity at
every state of the justice system.

Removing barriers that make it harder for
individuals with criminal records to turn their lives
around.

During cries for equality in our criminal justice system, we
often hear calls for peace. However, as Dr. King reminds
us, "True peace is not merely the absence of tension: it is
the presence of justice."[32]

No wonder so many cry out today, "No justice, no peace."

International Rates of Incarceration per 100,000

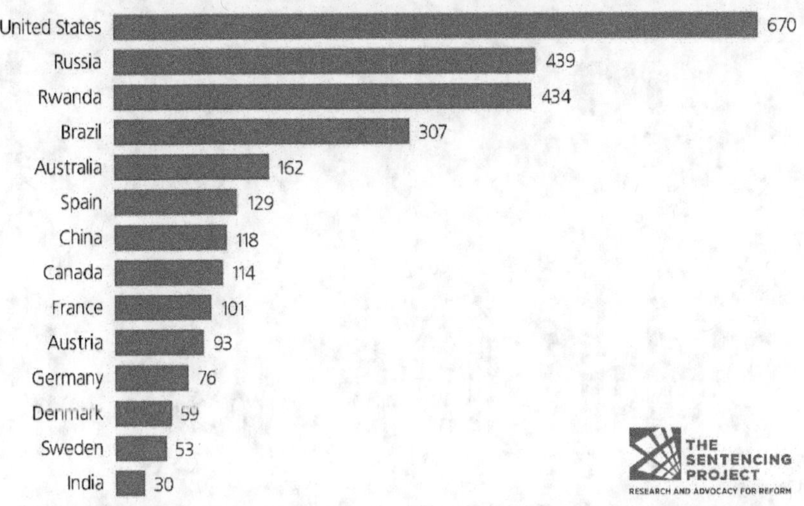

Source: Walmsley, R. (2016). *World Prison Brief*. London: Institute for Criminal Policy Research. Available online: http://www.prisonstudies.org/world-prison-brief.

U.S. State and Federal Prison Population, 1925-2015

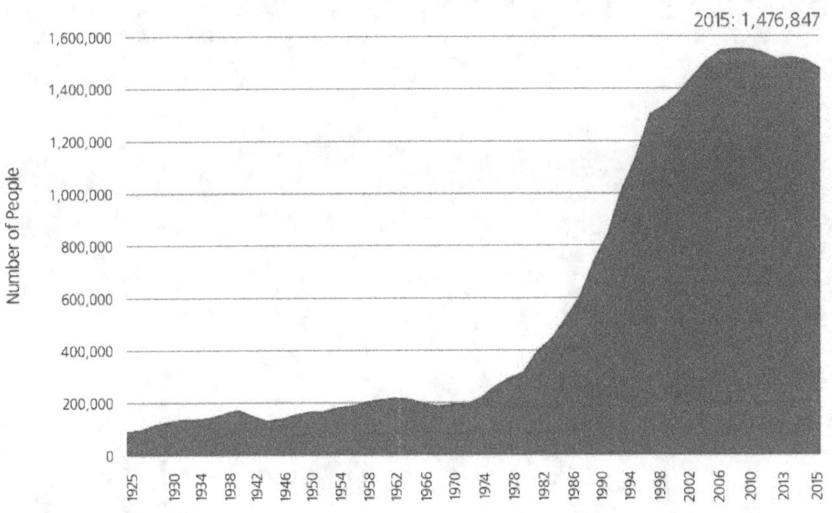

Source: Bureau of Justice Statistics *Prisoners Series*.

Lifetime Likelihood of Imprisonment of U.S. Residents Born in 2001

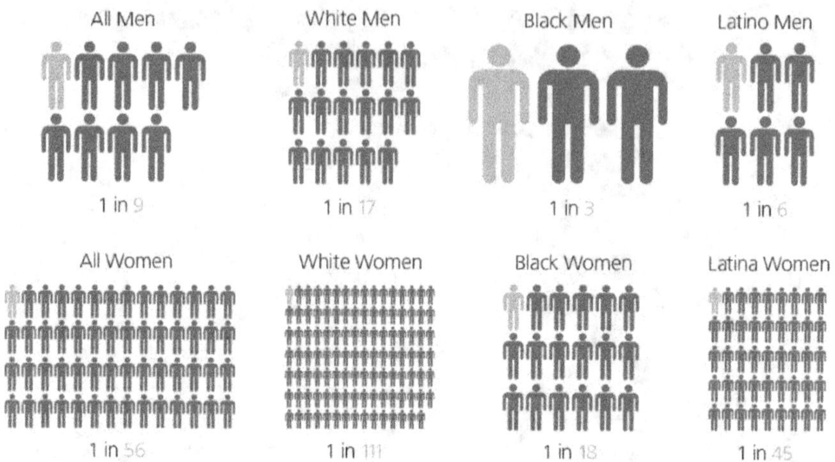

Source: Bonczar, T. (2003). *Prevalence of Imprisonment in the U.S. Population, 1974-2001*. Washington, DC: Bureau of Justice Statistics.

Number of People in Prisons and Jails for Drug Offenses, 1980 and 2015

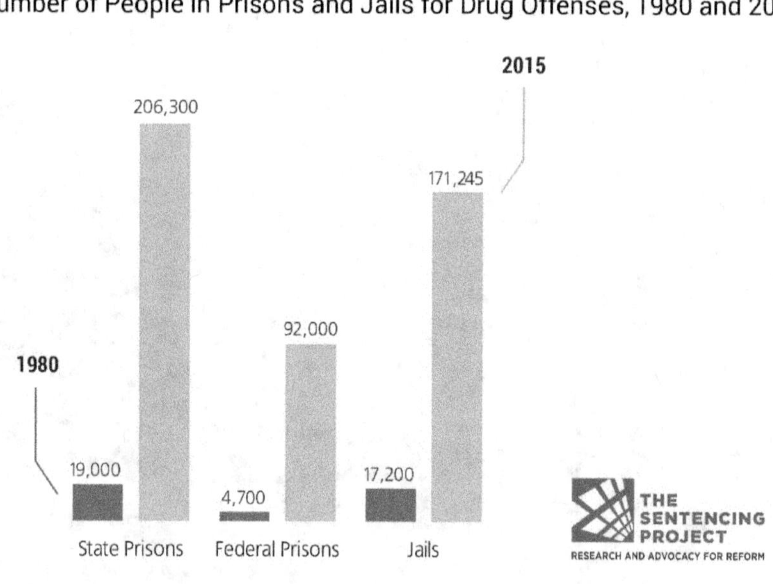

Sources: Carson, E.A. and Anderson, E. (2016). *Prisoners in 2015*. Washington, DC: Bureau of Justice Statistics; James, D.J. (2004). *Profile of Jail Inmates, 2002*. Washington, DC: Bureau of Justice Statistics; Mauer, M. and King, R. (2007). *A 25-Year Quagmire: The War on Drugs and its Impact on American Society*. Washington, DC: The Sentencing Project; Minton, T.D. and Zeng, Z. (2016). Jail Inmates in 2015. Washington, DC: Bureau of Justice Statistics.

Police Brutality (Black Lives Matter)

We can never be satisfied as long as the Negro is the victim of the unspeakable horrors of police brutality.

I offer a grade of C for this dream. An objective look at the horrors at the hands of police during Dr. King's time compared with today will show progress. However, as is the case for so many issues, there is much work to be done. One death is one too many.

Let me start by sharing that my brother is a former police officer, my neighbor is a City of Memphis police officer, and I have the highest respect for those who willingly put their lives on the line to serve and protect our communities. Although I served most of my adult life as a member of the US Navy, I've always believed that those who serve in a police uniform sacrifice just as much (if not more) than those of us in a military uniform.

Activist and author Jim Wallis shares similar thoughts in his book, *America's Original Sin*: "It's vital to acknowledge the many good police in our communities and to recognize that our police officers do a very difficult and dangerous job."[33]

Likewise, President Obama noted that officers who serve their communities "deserve our respect and gratitude every single day. Tonight, I ask people to reject violence and words that harm, and turn to words that heal—prayer, patient dialogue, and sympathy for the friends and family of the fallen."[34]

In 2014, 126 officers died in the line of duty—50 from firearms-related incidents, 49 from traffic-related incidents, and 27 from other causes, of which 24 were from job-related illnesses such as heart attacks.[35]

Respecting the good work of our police officers does not take away the need for change. Nor does the fact that many of us have positive experiences with police officers negate the need for all of us to acknowledge wrongdoings and take steps to make all our citizens feel safe, protected, and served by our law enforcement officials.

This is an area in which many leaders agree. "Conservative white Southern Baptist leader Russell Moore said this in the wake of Ferguson: 'In the public arena, we ought to recognize that it is empirically true that African-American men are more likely, by virtually every measure, to be arrested, sentenced, executed, or murdered than their white peers. We cannot shrug that off with apathy. Working toward justice in this arena will mean consciences that are sensitive to the problem. But how can we get there when white people do not face the same experiences as do black people?'"[36]

Unfortunately, not a lot of information is known about this troubling issue. What little is known shows a disparity in the way that African Americans are treated relative to their population. For example, "African Americans represent 31 percent of deaths by law enforcement officers reported to the FBI in 2012 while making up only 13 percent of the US population."[37]

We need to learn much more if we're going to make a difference in the lives of those most affected by this tragedy. Congressman Steve Cohen (D-TN), who represents Memphis, introduced a bill that would mandate tracking data about the shooting of civilians by law enforcement. "It is ridiculous that we can't tell the American people how many lives were ended by police officers this year, or any year. Before we can truly address the problem of excessive force used by law enforcement we have to understand the nature of the problem and that begins with accurate data. That is why I introduced the National Statistics on Deadly Force Act; so that our country can do a better job of honestly assessing racial disparities and other problems in our justice system and begin to fix them."[38]

I agree that to root out the cause of police brutality, we need to better understand the issue from all sides. However, we cannot sit idly by waiting for more information while our neighbors are being abused or killed by those who are sworn to protect and serve. We cannot let a lack of accurate data justify apathy. Just because the issue may not affect us personally or those we care about, it doesn't mean that we have no responsibility to help those who are affected.

This leads me to one of the groups trying to make a difference—a group whose name can create controversy through a misunderstanding of their purpose and practices. According to their website, "#Black Lives Matter is a unique contribution that goes beyond extrajudicial killings of Black people by police and vigilantes. Black Lives Matter is an ideological and political intervention in a world where Black lives are systematically and intentionally targeted for demise. It is an affirmation of Black folks' contributions to this society, our humanity, and our resilience in the face of deadly oppression. We are committed to embodying and practicing justice, liberation, and peace in our engagements with one another. We are committed to collectively, lovingly, and courageously working vigorously for freedom and justice for Black people, and by extension, all people. As we forge our path we intentionally build and nurture a beloved community that is bonded together through a beautiful struggle that is restorative, not depleting."[39]

I spoke with my daughter about Black Lives Matter, and she offered this perspective:

> I think it's a good organization because, honestly, as a young person and a white person, I didn't know these issues still went on. I thought it was just in the '60s. I thought we were way past that. So, as a white person, I didn't see racism that much, and I was kind of ignorant to it. I definitely didn't think that police, of all people, would ever be doing something like this. I couldn't believe that police would target someone because of the color of their skin, but then there was a second and a third [incident], and it keeps going on. And now there are videos that force you to realize exactly what's going on. People are not doing anything wrong, and they're still being shot and killed. So, I think somebody had to stand up and do something. Black Lives, the organization, are putting information out through the media so people are finally like, "We have to do something,"

because white people just don't realize it's going on because they don't see it themselves.[40]

She added that some people view Black Lives Matters as "antiwhite. They say, 'What about all lives?' But 'all lives' aren't the ones getting shot and killed by police. So, we need to be focused on black lives right now."[41]

Some will respond to a cry like "Black Lives Matter" with something like "All Lives Matter" or "Blue Lives Matter." Of course, all lives matter, and by extension, blue lives (police officers) matter, too. But that misses the point of the struggle. It ignores that problem that exists in our society today.

I gained a better understanding of this concept while watching Larry Wilmore interview comedian Felonious Munk, who said, "If I break my leg, I do not want the doctor telling me, 'All legs should be healed.' I want the doctor to fix *my* leg." The discussion continued with Wilmore asking, "You're saying 'Black lives matter' is a specific cry for something, whereas 'All lives matter' is a non sequitur?" Munk responded, "There's not a sequitur to be found, Brother Larry. One does not attend a reading by Toni Morrison and interrupt her to say, 'Yes, but why have you not weighed in on the movie *Minions*?'"[42]

This is an example I share with my college students, when we discuss media coverage of this issue. I remind them that a statement such as "Black lives matter" is not a disparagement against other lives. It's an acknowledgment about a real issue that affects our brothers and sisters of color in this nation. It's an issue that all of us should care about. It's an issue that we must continue to struggle for if we're ever going to make real progress for the "victim of the unspeakable horrors of police brutality."[43]

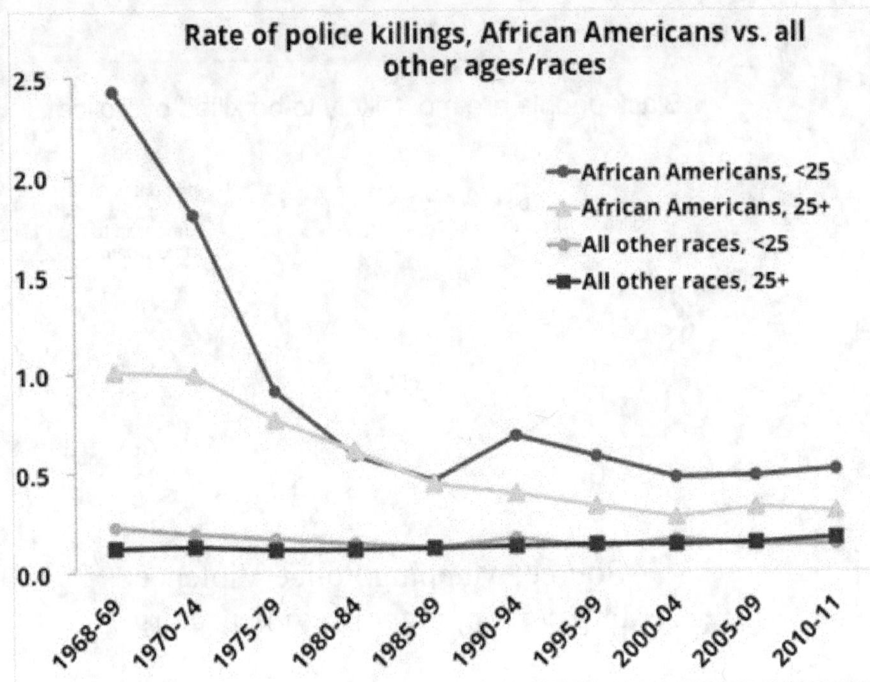

Source: Center on Juvenile and Criminal Justice,
http://www.cjcj.org/news/8113

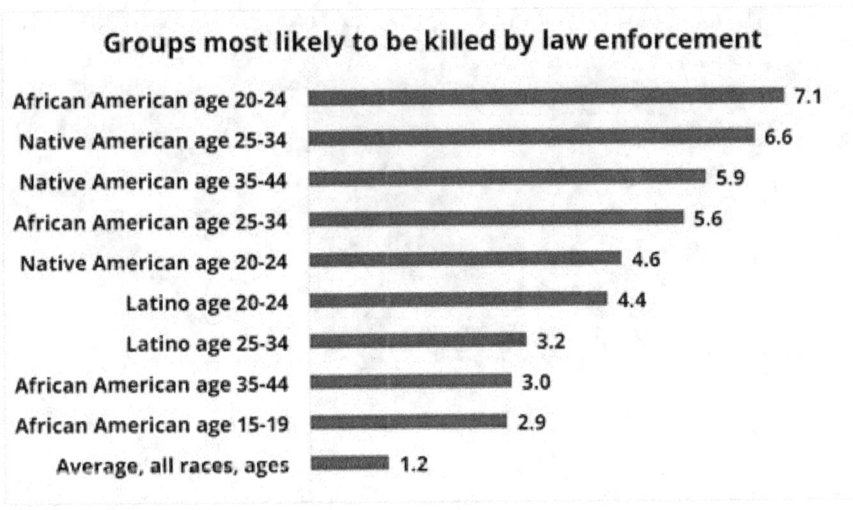

Source: Center on Juvenile and Criminal Justice,
http://www.cjcj.org/news/8113

Black people are most likely to be killed by police

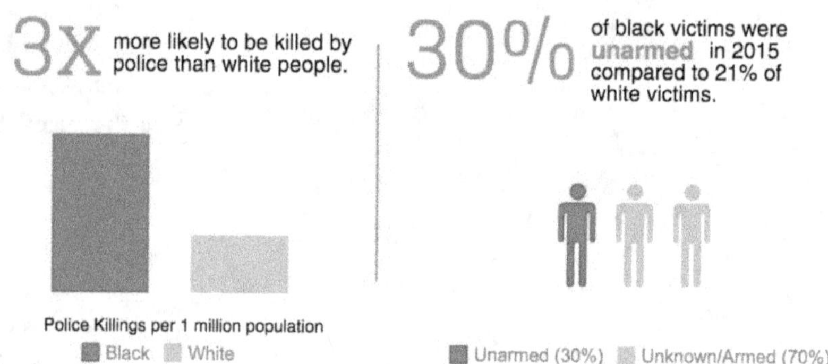

Source: Mapping Police Violence,
https://mappingpoliceviolence.org/

It's not about crime

Fewer than 1 in 3 black people killed by police in America in 2014 were suspected of a violent crime and allegedly armed.

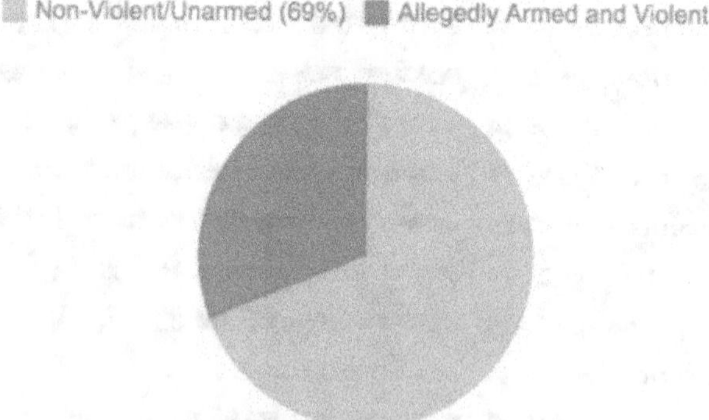

Source: Mapping Police Violence,
https://mappingpoliceviolence.org/

There are proven solutions

Police Departments that have adopted these use of force policies kill significantly fewer people. But few departments have adopted them.

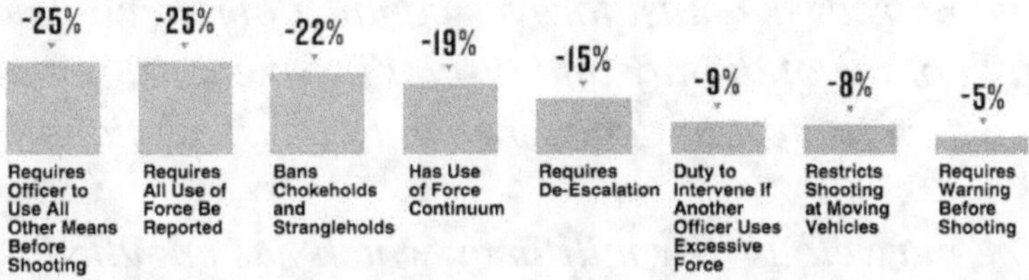

Source: Mapping Police Violence, https://mappingpoliceviolence.org/

The Right of the People to Peaceably Assemble

In the process of gaining our rightful place we must not be guilty of wrongful deeds. Let us not seek to satisfy our thirst for freedom by drinking from the cup of bitterness and hatred. We must forever conduct our struggle on the high plane of dignity and discipline. We must not allow our creative protest to degenerate into physical violence.

The marvelous new militancy which has engulfed the Negro community must not lead us to a distrust of all white people, for many of our white brothers, as evidenced by their presence here today, have come to realize that their destiny is tied up with our destiny. They have come to realize that their freedom is inextricably bound to our freedom. We cannot walk alone.

I offer a grade of B– for this dream. I base this on a comparison of protest responses in Dr. King's time with those seen today.

When Dr. King accepted the Nobel Peace Prize in 1964, he said, "World peace through nonviolent means is neither absurd nor unattainable. All other methods have failed. Thus we must begin anew. Nonviolence is a good starting point. Those of us who believe in this method can be voices of reason, sanity, and understanding amid the voices of violence, hatred, and emotion. We can very well set a mood of peace out of which a system of peace can be built."[44]

The First Amendment of the US Constitution guarantees "the right of the people peaceably to assemble and to petition the Government for a redress of grievances."[45]

Few would argue that citizens have a right to protest, and most would acknowledge that physical violence hurts a cause more than it helps. The question is, what constitutes a peaceful protest? Does breaking the law, impeding traffic, for example, count as a peaceful protest? How about sitting at a *whites-only* lunch counter or refusing to move to the back of the bus?

On July 10, 2016, protestors shut down Hernando de Soto Bridge in Memphis. Traffic was stalled along I-40 across the Mississippi River for hours. Some argue that this was the largest civil rights protest in Memphis since the sanitation workers' strikes in 1968, a strike that Dr. King supported before his assassination in the city that same year.

According to Memphis journalist Wendi C. Thomas, "This loosely organized crowd resurrected the radical spirit of the exemplar of civil disobedience, Dr. Martin Luther King Jr., who was assassinated nearly 50 years ago, on a motel balcony not two miles from the bridge. He came to town on behalf of striking black city sanitation workers. Knowingly or not, the masses followed the instructions in one of King's last speeches here: Apply economic pressure to force the city to provide better-paying jobs and end economic apartheid."[46]

The bridge blockade ended with no arrests or violence. At one point, Memphis Police Director Michael Rallings linked arms with protestors and peacefully led many off the bridge.

The NAACP Memphis Chapter released this statement: "The NAACP stands with and fully supports the rights of The Black Lives Matter Movement and all citizens to gather in peaceful protest. The peaceful gathering demonstrates our awareness and disdain with the poor economic policies of our city and its priorities as well as the national sentiment towards injustices that permeate the disproportional contact between law enforcement and people of color. The Memphis Branch of the NAACP wishes to express gratitude to the men and women of The Memphis Police Department and the partner branches of law enforcement for exercising restraint under extreme pressure during tonight's peaceful protest."[47]

The Memphis protest is just one example of how citizens can exercise their right to protest peacefully, while technically breaking the law, without being arrested. I've heard some of my friends claim that they support peaceful protests as long as it doesn't break the law. While I can appreciate their point of view, I don't believe we should be surprised when laws are broken based on decades of unheard voices. As the "nation's apostle of nonviolence," Dr. King, once said, "A riot is the language of the unheard."[48]

How long can we expect our fellow citizens to endure the status quo before their cries for justice reach a level that can be heard by those not personally affected by the injustice? Sometimes it requires making others feel uncomfortable. Sometimes people will be inconvenienced, even if it means blocking traffic (technically against the law).

Others may be in a position to gain attention without breaking the law but instead violate what some believe are socially accepted norms. For example, "San Francisco quarterback, Colin Kaepernick, willingly immersed himself into controversy by refusing to stand for the playing of the national anthem in protest of what he deems are wrongdoings against African Americans and minorities in the United States."[49]

"I am not going to stand up to show pride in a flag for a country that oppresses black people and people of color," Kaepernick told NFL Media in an exclusive interview after the game. "To me, this is bigger than football and it would be selfish on my part to look the other way. There are bodies in the street and people getting paid leave and getting away with murder."[50]

While talking with my son-in-law, who serves in the air force, he mentioned that Kaepernick's protest is "publicly televised where a lot of people see what he's doing. This makes a much bigger impact than anything else he could do. He's not being violent. It's 100 percent peaceful, and he's not even interrupting anything. Yes, we're in the military, but we fight for his right to do that, and we should respect that."[51]

While teaching a lesson about patriotism, one of my college students stated his objection to what Kaepernick had done. I asked why, and the student replied that as a retired military veteran, he believed that Kaepernick was disrespecting what the national anthem stood for. I asked what he thought the national anthem stood for, and without hesitation the student replied, "Freedom." So I asked how he defined freedom. The student thought for a moment and said that he felt like freedom was being able to do what you want as long as it doesn't hurt someone else. I agreed and asked if that freedom could include someone who chooses to make a statement by refusing to stand for the national anthem. Silence.

It was a good opportunity to look at peaceful protest from a different perspective. I know I've had to do the same after I've made a rash judgment based on incomplete media reports. I know better than to prejudge something before I understand all sides, and yet time and again, I must confess that I'm guilty—guilty of pronouncing judgment against a person or a group of people before trying to understand, or at least appreciate, their viewpoint. As a person who wore the cloth of our nation for more than two decades, I owe it to myself and those protected by the Constitution I swore to protect and defend to support those exercising their right to peaceably assemble.

I would like to think that I can serve as an example of a white person who has "come to realize that [my] destiny is tied up with [their] destiny." That I "have come to realize that [my] freedom is inextricably bound to [their] freedom." If I'm honest, I know I still have a lot to learn, and plenty of room to grow; however, I do know for certain that "we cannot walk alone."[52]

A seventeen-year-old civil rights demonstrator being attacked by a police dog during protests in Birmingham, Alabama, in May 1963. (Source: Associated Press)

Firefighters turn their hoses full force on civil rights demonstrators on July 15, 1963, in Birmingham, Alabama. (Source: *Time*)

Interim Police Director Michael Rallings leads protestors off the Hernando de Soto Bridge on July 10, 2016, in Memphis, Tennessee. (Source: WREG-TV)

Ieshia Evans stands silently before a line of heavily armed cops on July 9, 2016, in Baton Rouge, Louisiana. (Source: Reuters)

Democracy (Disenfranchisement)

Now is the time to make real the promises of democracy.

I offer a grade of C– for this dream primarily based on laws passed in many states that disenfranchise voters of color through voter identification requirements veiled under the auspices of so-called voter fraud—a claim that has been debunked by multiple studies and described by a federal appeals court as targeting "African-Americans with almost surgical precision."[53]

According to the Brennan Center for Justice at New York University School of Law, "a look at the facts makes clear fraud is vanishingly rare, and does not happen on a scale even close to that necessary to 'rig' an election."[54]

Most of the reports of voter fraud turn out to be the result of clerical errors or issues with bad data. The Brennan Center found that voter fraud occurred between 0.0003 and 0.0025 percent, meaning a person in America is more likely to be "struck by lightning than that he will impersonate another voter at the polls."[55]

According to Loyola Law School Professor Justin Levitt, whose research focuses on election administration, "A comprehensive investigation of voter impersonation finds 31 credible incidents out of one billion ballots cast."[56] Levitt has been tracking voter fraud allegations for years, and in 2008, he reviewed every single allegation before the Supreme Court. He doesn't just track prosecutions, but he also researches "any specific credible allegation that someone may have pretended to be someone else at the polls, in any way that an ID law could fix."[57]

Similarly, Columbia University political scientist Dr. Lorraine Minnite reported that voter fraud could generally be traced to "false claims by the loser of a close race, mischief and administrative or voter error."[58]

One of the key findings from the Columbia University study is especially germane:

> There is a long history in America of elites using voter fraud allegations to restrict and shape the electorate. In the late nineteenth century when newly freed black Americans were swept into electoral politics, and where blacks were the majority of the electorate, it was the Democrats who were threatened by a loss of power, and it was the Democratic party that erected new rules said to be necessary to respond to alleged fraud by black voters. Today, the success of voter registration drives among minorities and low income people in recent years threatens to expand the base of the Democratic party and tip the balance of power away from the Republicans. Consequently, the use of baseless voter fraud allegations for partisan advantage has become the exclusive domain of Republican party activists.[59]

Dr. Minnite also noted:

> The historically disenfranchised are often the target of voter fraud allegations. Fraud allegations today

typically point the finger at those belonging to the same categories of voters accused of fraud in the past—the marginalized and formerly disenfranchised, urban dwellers, immigrants, blacks, and lower status voters. These populations are mostly found among those still struggling for full inclusion in American life.[60]

Although the Voting Rights Act was passed just two years after Dr. King's "I Have a Dream" speech, progress has not consistently led to the real promises of democracy that many struggle for today.

Best-selling author and international commentator on ethics and public life Jim Wallis described how

> voting rights were won in 1965, but the tripartite strategy of denying the vote to returning prisoners, suppressing minority voting through new ID requirements, and the partisan gerrymandering of districts to "bleach" them white are all working together to deny black and brown Americans their voting rights as American citizens.[61]

Vanessa Perez, PhD, identified the following based on her research: "Rates of identification-ownership are highest among White individuals, while other ethnic groups disproportionately lack necessary photo ID. Thirteen percent of Blacks, 10 percent of Hispanics, but only 5 percent of Whites lack photographic identification."[62]

Some argue that requiring a photo ID is common sense, but most who make this argument already have a government-issued photo ID. What they really mean is that it's no big deal for them because they've never considered the impact it could have on those who do not have a government-issued photo ID. Nicol Turner-Lee offers this relevant observation: "More stringent photo identification requirements have become the 'poll tax' for more than 21 million Americans, or 11 percent of the entire voting-eligible population without government-issued photo IDs."[63] So, not only is a voter ID law an ineffective method for combating nearly nonexistent voter fraud, but these laws also hurt potential voters, a majority of whom are people of color.[64]

I believe that most could admit that much progress has been made since Dr. King delivered his, "I have a Dream" speech, when Jim Crow laws were still in effect. However, there is still much work to be done before we, "make real the promises of democracy."

Individuals with Confirmed ID by Ethnicity

	PERCENTAGE OF POPULATION	CONFIRMED ID	NO CONFIRMED ID
White	71%	95%	5%
Black	12%	87%	13%
Hispanic	11%	90%	10%
Other	6%	89%	11%
Don't Know	1%	49%	51%
Total	**100%**	**93%**	**7%**

Source: American National Elections Study, as cited in 2015
Project Vote Research Memo by Vanessa M. Perez, Ph.D.

Voting Rights (Gerrymandering)

We cannot be satisfied as long as a Negro in Mississippi cannot vote and a Negro in New York believes he has nothing for which to vote.

I give this dream a C.

Just like democracy and voter disenfranchisement, covered in a separate chapter, there are many issues that negatively affect voters of color.

One issue is an example of how Dr. King described a person who "believes he has nothing for which to vote." The issue is drawing congressional district lines in a way that benefits one group of people over another, which is commonly known as gerrymandering. The term was first used by the *Boston Gazette* in 1812. The *Washington Post* offered a visual guide to gerrymandering in March 2015.[65]

In 1985, the Supreme Court in a unanimous decision found "that a North Carolina redistricting plan unlawfully discriminated against blacks in six voting districts." In violation of the Voting Rights Act, this damaged the ability of black citizens "to participate equally in the political process and to elect candidates of their choice."[66]

Unfortunately, there are still too many cases today where a voter of color could "believe he has nothing for which to vote."

For example, on June 19, 2017, the Supreme Court "agreed to hear Wisconsin's appeal of a lower court ruling that found its 2011 state redistricting plan was unconstitutional due to partisan gerrymandering."

This is a case many will watch closely to judge whether we're moving closer or further away from the goal of ensuring an individual's vote in one district or state can have the same influence as an individual in another district or state. The Supreme Court decision could decide if one person, one vote means that everyone enjoys the right to choose their own representation in this democracy. This contrasts with how some describe gerrymandering today as politicians choosing their voters, instead of voters choosing their politicians.

Unlike the 1985 case which outlawed racial gerrymandering, the current case before the Supreme Court may decide whether state legislators can draw district lines based on partisan gerrymandering. While the focus will be on partisanship, the effect on a voter of color is the same, especially when one considers that an overwhelming majority of African Americans vote for politicians from the same party.

Disenfranchising voters of color goes beyond just gerrymandering. It also includes other changes in voting policy such as the number of days allowed for early voting, ID requirements, and the number and location of polling places. Beginning with the Voting Rights Act of 1965, voters were protected in part from nefarious changes in voting rules by state legislators because those changes required federal approval.

In 2013, the Supreme Court ruled that states could change their election laws without advance federal approval. According to many, this decision diminished the effectiveness of the landmark Voting Rights Act of 1965.[67]

In her dissent, Justice Ruth Bader Ginsburg expressed her disagreement with the decision citing the words of Dr. King and writing that his legacy and the nation's commitment to justice had been "disserved by today's decision."[68]

Justice Ginsburg said, "The focus of the Voting Rights Act had properly changed from 'first-generation barriers to ballot access' to 'second-generation barriers' like racial gerrymandering and laws requiring at-large voting in places with a sizable black minority."[69]

Justice Ginsburg referred to Dr. King describing how "the great man who led the march from Selma to Montgomery and there called for the passage of the Voting Rights Act foresaw progress, even in Alabama. 'The arc of the moral universe is long,' he said, but 'it bends toward justice,' if there is a steadfast commitment to see the task through to completion."[70]

As citizens of this great democracy, I believe we have a responsibility to see this task to completion. This task includes ensuring the rights of *all* men and women to vote and developing an election system in which *all* men and women believe they have something "for which to vote."

Gerrymandering, explained

Three different ways to divide 50 people into five districts

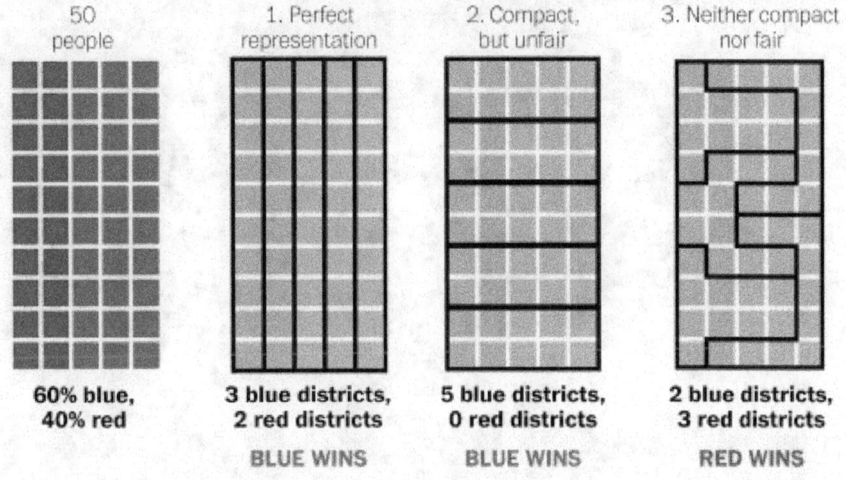

Gerrymandering Explained

Current congressional district map

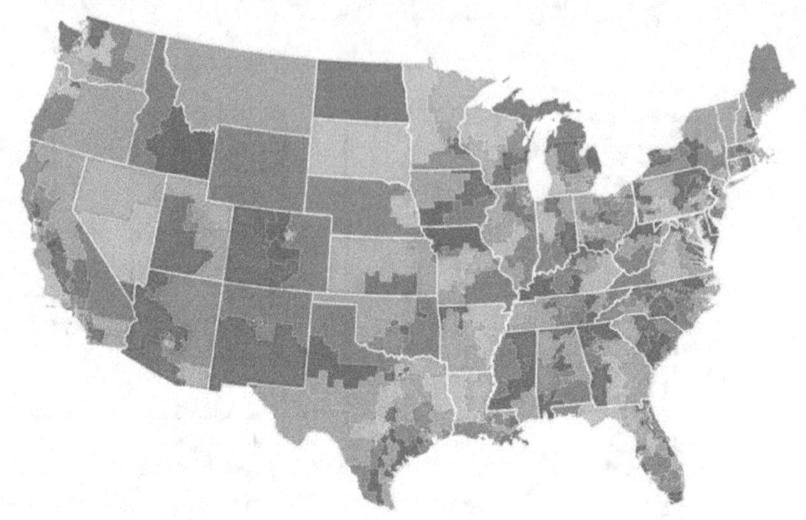

Computer-drawn map to optimize compactness

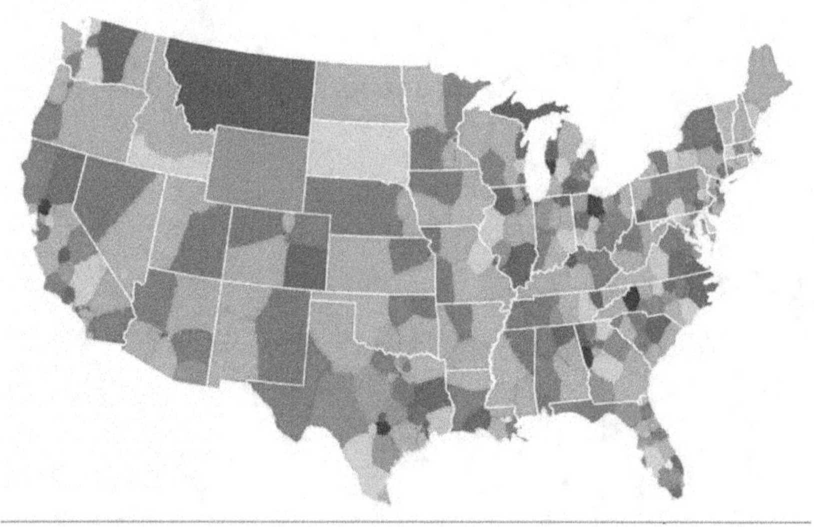

Economic Opportunity (Economic Reality)

We cannot be satisfied as long as the Negro's basic mobility is from a smaller ghetto to a larger one.

I give this a grade of C– because, while the economic *opportunity* for people of color may have increased since Dr. King's 1963 speech, the economic *reality* is not good for most.

For example, in 2011, median household income for a white family was $67,175, compared to $40,007 for a Latino family and $39,760 for a black family.[71] There are many reasons for this that I'll leave to others more qualified to parse, but suffice it to say that there is not economic equality in a society where one race enjoys an annual income nearly twice as much as another race. While wages of white families are nearly twice as much as those of their black counterparts, an even more staggering statistic is that a white family's net worth is more than ten times that of a black family.

According to a 2013 Pew Research Center study, the median net worth of white households was $141,900, compared to $13,700 for Latino households and $11,000 for black households.[72] This creates all kinds of consequences that exasperate inequality in our society—the ability to attend college or a trade school, start a small business, or pursue just about anything else that offers an opportunity to climb the economic ladder of success but requires an up-front expense. It also hurts those trying to avoid debt but often have no choice for unexpected health issues, car repairs, or any other financial crisis. The consequences of a net worth gap also affect those who wish to own a home, which usually requires a significant down payment.

It's no wonder that in 2013 the home-ownership rate for white households was 73.9 percent, compared to 47.4 percent for minority households.[73] Of course, home ownership (or lack thereof) can lead to even greater economic gaps between the haves and the have-nots.

The flip side of wealth is poverty, and that, too, is felt unevenly in our society. For example, between 2007 and 2011, there were 42.7 million people, or 14.3 percent of the US population, living below the poverty level.[74] The wealthiest nation on earth should not have one out of seven of its citizens living in poverty. It's even more tragic when we consider that 8.9 percent of white (non-Hispanic) people live in poverty compared with 25.8 percent of black or African Americans live in poverty.[75]

Part of the disparity in poverty rates can be traced to disparity in the job market. A quote from the White House archives offers a good assessment of the African American unemployment rate: "While the unemployment rate for African Americans has fallen below its pre-recession average, more work remains to close long-standing disparities in the labor market. Nevertheless, the current African-American unemployment rate—8.8 percent as of January 2016—remains too high,"[76]

A starker contrast can be observed when "looking at the changes in employment by race between 2007 and 2013, [where] we see that black men have almost double the unemployment rate of their white counterparts. At almost 14 percent, this is actually significantly higher than all of the other categories."[77]

Of course, income, wealth, poverty, and home-ownership gaps are not unique to American capitalism; however, the disparity between white citizens and citizens of color is staggering. This often leads to what Dr. King described as moving from "one smaller ghetto to a larger one."[78]

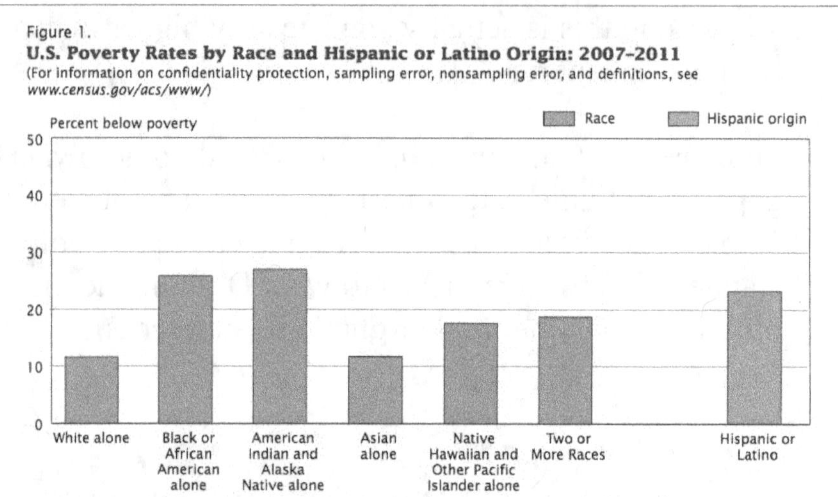

US Poverty Rates by Race and Hispanic or Latino Origin, 2007–2011

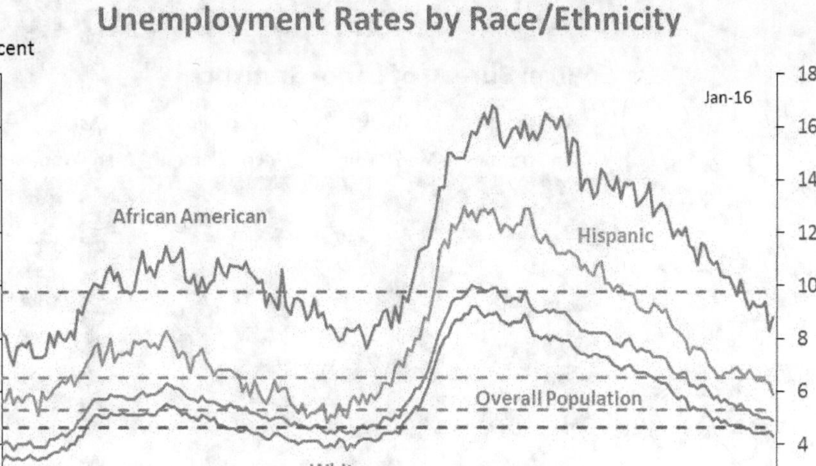

Unemployment Rates by Race/Ethnicity

The jobs crisis by race and gender

Source: Bureau of Labor Statistics

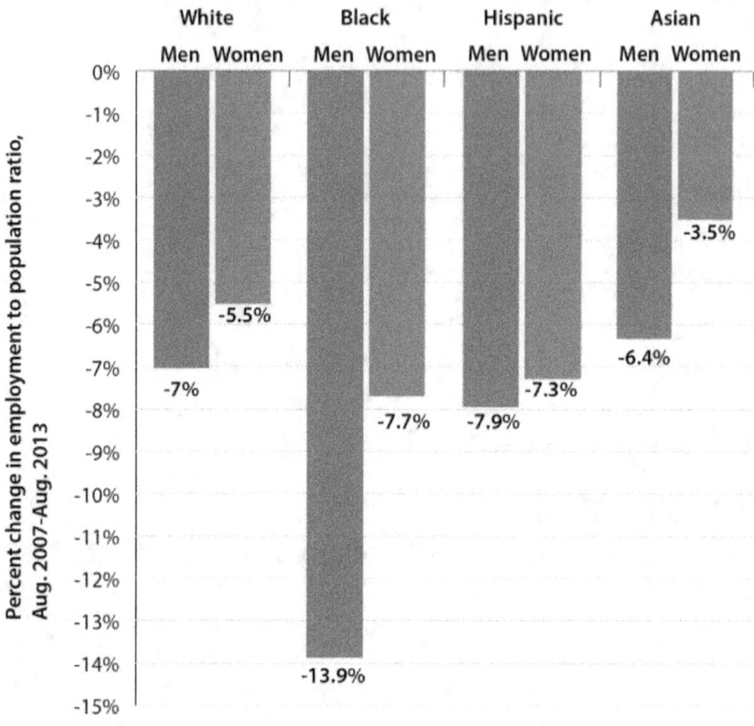

The Jobs Crisis by Race and Gender

Equal Access (Public Accommodation)

We can never be satisfied, as long as our bodies, heavy with the fatigue of travel, cannot gain lodging in the motels of the highways and the hotels of the cities.

We can never be satisfied as long as our children are stripped of their selfhood and robbed of their dignity by signs stating "For Whites Only."

I give this a grade of B+ because I believe this is the dream where we've made significant progress. To fully appreciate the progress made, it's helpful to review where the nation was before equal access to public accommodation was the law of the land.

Let's start with what Dr. King described as the inability to "gain lodging in the motels of the highways and the hotels of the cities."[79]

Many may not remember, but in 1963, there were many places in our nation where "blacks could not use restaurants, bathrooms, water fountains, public parks, beaches, or swimming pools used by whites. They had to use separate entrances to doctor's offices and sit in separate waiting rooms. They could only sit in the balcony or in other designated areas of theaters. They had to ride at the back of streetcars and buses."[80]

At the time of Dr. King's "I Have a Dream" speech, many African Americans used a guide called *The Negro Travelers' Green Book*, also referred to as the *Green Book*.[81]

It was in publication from 1936 until 1964, when the Civil Rights Act was passed. The book included hotels, restaurants, and other establishments that served blacks. This was very important during a time when segregation was common and legally enforceable through Jim Crow laws. Not only was travel a challenge for African Americans, but it was also frequently dangerous. In 1949, the eighty-page book cost $0.75, and the cover included a quote by Mark Twain: "Travel is fatal to prejudice."[82]

This excerpt from the 1956 guide offers a peek into the disparity between white and black travelers: "The white traveler has had no difficulty in getting accommodations, but with the Negro it has been different. He, before the advent of a Negro travel guide, had to depend on word of mouth, and many times accommodations were not available."[83]

Victor H. Green published the book to "save the travelers of his race as many difficulties and embarrassments as possible."[84] This quaint introduction to the *Green Book* reminds me of some of the ways in which we tend to overlook or minimize the real danger that affects people of color in our society. It was, and still is, more than just "difficult" or "embarrassing" for many African Americans to enjoy equal access to public accommodation. There were, and to a lesser extent still are, instances in which African Americans are in danger when exercising their rights to access public accommodations.

Green predicted that "there will be a day sometime in the near future when this guide will not have to be published. That is when we as a race will have equal opportunities and privileges in the United States."[85] The final edition of the *Green Book* was published in 1964, the same year that Congress passed the Civil Rights Act prohibiting discrimination in public places.[86]

The *Green Book* is part of our history, and legally, people of color have equal access to public accommodation, but additional progress remains to be made in this area. Just because one has legal access to public accommodation, it does not mean that the person has real equal access to public accommodation. For several economic and social reasons, many people of color still do not truly enjoy access to accommodation in all public settings.

The dream of equal access to public accommodation has not been fully achieved. The "For Whites Only" signs have been removed, but there are still some who are treated differently based on the color of their skin. I explore this further in the chapter devoted to content of character and white privilege.

The Negro Motorist Green Book promised safer travel without embarrassment.

Segregation protesters Professor John R. Salter, Joan Trunpauer, and Annie Moody remain at a sit-in at a lunch counter in Jackson, Mississippi, even after Professor Salter was sprayed with condiments and beaten on the back and head by spectators in the crowd, May 28, 1963. (Source: Getty Images)

Protestors in Cairo, Illinois, carry signs protesting African Americans during racial unrest circa 1960.
(Source: Abraham Lincoln Presidential Library and Museum)

Teenagers take part in what became known as the Children's March on May 2, 1963, in Birmingham, Alabama.
(Source: Alabama Public Radio)

A pro-segregation rally at the Arkansas State Capitol in Little Rock, protesting the integration of schools such as Little Rock's Central High School in 1957. (Source: History Channel)

Faith (Church Diversity)

I have a dream that one day on the red hills of Georgia the sons of former slaves and the sons of former slave owners will be able to sit down together at the table of brotherhood.

With this faith we will be able to transform the jangling discords of our nation into a beautiful symphony of brotherhood. With this faith we will be able to work together, to pray together, to struggle together, to go to jail together, to stand up for freedom together, knowing that we will be free one day.

I'm offering a grade of D for this dream. Unlike many of the dreams that are hindered by institutional bias, this one depends primarily on individual choice based on our own personal biases.

Listening to Dr. King talk about faith during his 1963 "I Have a Dream" speech, I was reminded of another quote from a sermon he preached at Atlanta's Ebenezer Baptist Church in 1953: "I am [ashamed] and appalled that eleven o'clock on Sunday morning is the most segregated hour in Christian America."[87]

I know from personal experience as a Christian who moved frequently during military service, most of the churches we attended lacked diversity and many rarely had any visitors, much less members, from a different race. My own experience is consistent with the findings of Jim Wallis who wrote that "the more choices people have—for instance, a larger number of congregations within a religious tradition to consider—the more people choose to worship with people who are racially like themselves."[88]

There are many possible reasons for why people of faith choose to self-segregate, but choosing to be around others who look, act, and think like us is not limited to Sunday morning.

"Fifty years after the great victories of the civil rights movement, and Dr. King's dramatic reminder that Sunday morning at eleven o'clock was the nation's most segregated hour, most Americans still live most of their lives segregated from other races. It is the geography of race that continues to separate us, keeping us in different neighborhoods, schools, and churches and keeping us from talking more deeply together and developing the empathy and relationships that bring understanding, friendships, common citizenship, and even spiritual fellowship."[89]

Sadly, the words of Dr. King from his April 16, 1963, letters from a Birmingham jail still ring true today. "But the judgment of God is upon the church as never before. If today's church does not recapture the sacrificial spirit of the early church, it will lose its authenticity, forfeit the loyalty of millions, and be dismissed as an irrelevant social club with no meaning for the twentieth century. Every day I meet young people whose disappointment with the church has turned into outright disgust."[90]

The experiences of young people that Dr. King described in 1963 continue with trends observed today. "Today, young adults ages 18 to 29 are less than half as likely to be white Christians as seniors age 65 and older. Nearly 7 in

10 American seniors (67 percent) are white Christians, compared to fewer than 3 in 10 (29 percent) young adults."[91]

"The chart below reveals just how quickly the proportions of white, non-Hispanic Christians have declined across generations. It shows the decline of white Christians among each successive generation."[92]

"There is some progress, and at least a motivation among key white evangelical leaders, to take seriously the demands of addressing centuries of racial inequality."[93]

"The key decision for (churches with multiracial congregations) was that, as the areas were changing around them, they decided to stay put and be committed to being a neighborhood church, regardless of the racial and ethnic composition of the neighborhood."[94]

One of the many things we love about our current church is the diversity that's apparent as soon as you walk in the door. Church leaders have a vision for the Life Church where "We are one church in many locations—dynamic, Spirit-filled and diverse—serving people, developing leaders and impacting generations." One of the Life Church's ten values is focused on diversity. "We are committed to experiencing life as a diverse community. We celebrate all cultures, races, personalities, ages and backgrounds because each reflects the beauty of our Maker in a unique way. Our differences individually complete us corporately."[95]

This kind of diversity does not happen by accident, just as our membership at the Life Church did not happen by accident. We purposely sought out a church in Memphis that offered diversity. We wanted to worship in a place that reflected the multiracial tapestry that makes Memphis a wonderfully vibrant and culturally rich city.

Our campus pastor, Johnny Hill, echoed similar desires: "I had diversity everywhere except church. I remember [in college] wanting a church that had diversity. That was one of the things when I was venting to a friend of mine about church. I was like, I want to be part of a church where black people and white people, Asian, Hispanic, whatever. Everybody can feel like they can fit in."[96]

"I would say in our church, it's completely true [diversity], but I have to remember when I leave church that not everybody thinks the way we think and not everybody feels the way we feel."[97]

"I feel like there is progress, but obviously there is still work to be done. You see it when things like some of the police shootings happen. You see the underlying things in people's hearts that are below the surface. It's like we're walking hand in hand, and I don't care about race, but then you see something on social media that kind of shows what's in their heart. Maybe you do care about race more than you thought you did, or maybe you do buy into racial stereotypes more than you thought you did, on either side."[98]

Because diversity does not happen naturally, it's not surprising to learn that there is not much diversity in most houses of worship in America today. According to a 2010 random sample of more than eleven thousand US congregations of different faith traditions, only 13.7

percent were considered multiracial.[99] There is some good news in this figure, however, because it represents a growth from 1998 when 7.4 percent of US congregations were multiracial.[100]

For church leaders who wish to grow in a way that reflects the increasing diversity of America, Michael Emerson offers a "20 percent rule."[101] According to his research, a group must reach 20 percent of an organization's total membership before cultural change can take place. This makes sense intuitively because there must be a core group that reaches critical mass before the rest of the group will hear and take seriously the concerns of that smaller group. There's also data to support the 20 percent rule. According to Emerson, the probability of contact between groups is 99 percent when another group reaches the 20 percent threshold.[102]

Having at least 20 percent of church membership comprise a different race is a nice measurable goal to achieve, but it's not enough. According to North Park University professor Soong-Chan Rah, "Churches have to move from welcoming diverse newcomers to sharing life with them. It's not just getting people sitting in the same room on Sundays."[103] In other words, a pastor at the pulpit can't be satisfied with seeing different shades of faces looking back from the pews. The pastor must encourage followers to fellowship with others where they live, not just where they worship.

Religious Affiliation by Age

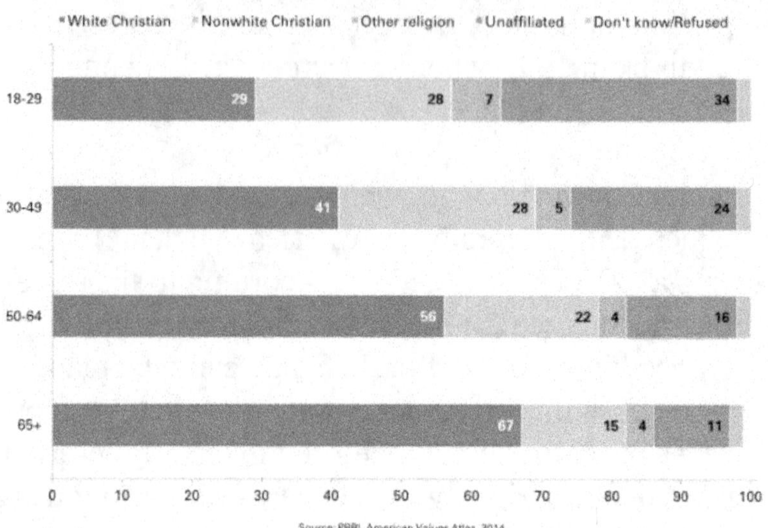

Marriage Equality (Interracial)

I have a dream that one day, down in Alabama, with its vicious racists, with its governor having his lips dripping with the words of interposition and nullification; one day right there in Alabama, little black boys and black girls will be able to join hands with little white boys and white girls as sisters and brothers.

I offer an A– for this dream.

Although Dr. King did not talk about marriage as part of his dream, I believe it's an issue that could be inferred from his dream that "little black boys and black girls will be able to join hands with little white boys and white girls as sisters and brothers."[104]

For the purposes of this writing, I will offer thoughts on marriage equality as it relates to the freedom that people have to marry between races. This is something many of us take for granted, myself included. In the interest of full disclosure, my wife of nearly thirty years is Mexican American, and our son-in-law is African American.

The same year my wife was born, an important Supreme Court decision legalized interracial marriage. In 1967, the Supreme Court ruled in *Loving v. Virginia* that couples could not be denied the right to marry regardless of their race. At the time, many states forbade marriage across racial lines.

According to the Pew Research Center, 17 percent of new marriages were interracial in 2015, compared with 3 percent in 1967. In other words, "one-in-six newlyweds are married to someone of a different race or ethnicity."[105] "More broadly, one-in-ten married people in 2015—not just those who *recently* married—had a spouse of a different race or ethnicity. This translates into 11 million people who were intermarried."[106]

There's also a change in attitude about interracial marriage. "Among adults who are not black, there's a shrinking share of those who say they would be opposed to having a close relative marrying someone who is black— from 63 percent in 1990, to 14 percent in 2016. Among those who are not white, the share opposed to a relative marrying a white person has dropped from 7 percent to 4 percent."[107]

Statistics are only part of the story. Just like every issue, it's easy to focus too much on the data and miss the impact that is felt on individuals.

While discussing the issue of interracial marriage with my campus pastor, Johnny Hill, he shared some of his own experiences as an African American man married to a white woman.

"Over time, I found that part of my heart completely opened up, and I felt like I could marry whoever God has for me. When it comes to marriage, I feel like we can be a bridge for others. When they see us happy, it can speak volumes to people. At the Life Church, we have all kinds of people here. When people pull up our church website, and they see me and Ashley, I believe God has put us in a position to be a voice, even in a time when things can be hostile."[108]

Although I focused on interracial marriage as part of this chapter, it is interesting to note that in 1998, Coretta Scott King addressed the lesbian, gay, bisexual, and transgender (LGBT) group Lambda Legal in Chicago. In her speech, she said, "I still hear people say that I should not be talking about the rights of lesbian and gay people and I should stick to the issue of racial justice. But I hasten to remind them that Martin Luther King Jr. said, 'Injustice anywhere is a threat to justice everywhere.' I appeal to everyone who believes in Martin Luther King Jr.'s dream to make room at the table of brother- and sisterhood for lesbian and gay people."[109]

In an April 1, 1998, *Chicago Tribune* article, Ms. King is also quoted as saying, "For many years now, I have been an outspoken supporter of civil and human rights for gay and lesbian people. Gays and lesbians stood up for civil rights in Montgomery, Selma, in Albany, Ga. and St. Augustine, Fla., and many other campaigns of the Civil Rights Movement. Many of these courageous men and women were fighting for my freedom at a time when they could find few voices for their own, and I salute their contributions."[110]

Finally, some note that openly gay civil rights leader Bayard Rustin was a special assistant to Dr. King and played a major role in organizing the march on Washington, where Dr. King delivered his "I Have a Dream" speech in August 1963. According to author Jerald Podair, "King resisted calls to jettison Rustin because he was gay."[111]

Since 1967, a steady rise in intermarriage in the U.S.

% who are intermarried among ...

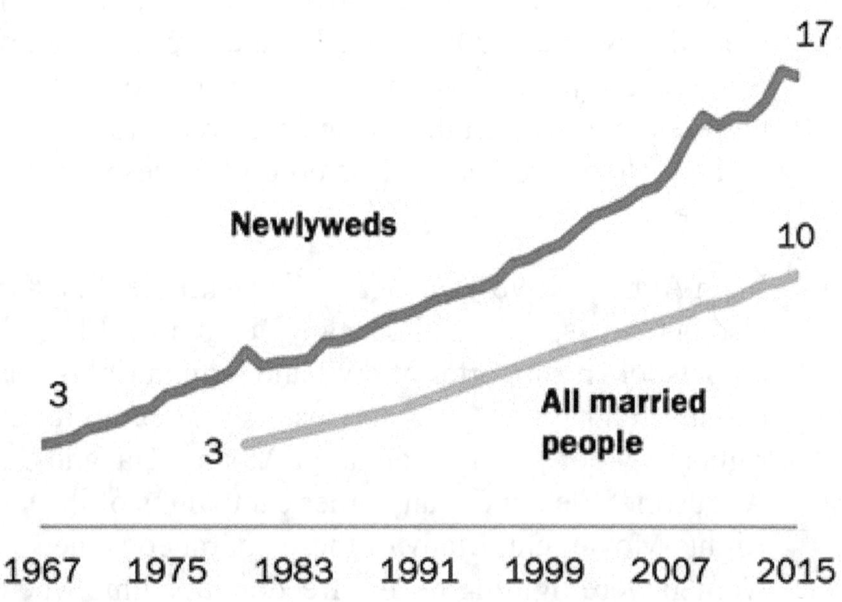

Note: Data prior to 1980 are estimates. See Methodology for more details. For "all married people," 1980, 1990, 2000, and 2008-2015 data points are shown.
Source: Pew Research Center analysis of 2008-2015 American Community Survey and 1980, 1990 and 2000 decennial censuses (IPUMS).
"Intermarriage in the U.S. 50 Years After Loving v. Virginia"

PEW RESEARCH CENTER

Conclusion: Will We Ever Be Free at Last?

And when this happens, when we allow freedom to ring, when we let it ring from every village and every hamlet, from every state and every city, we will be able to speed up that day when all of God's children, black men and white men, Jews and Gentiles, Protestants and Catholics, will be able to join hands and sing in the words of the old Negro spiritual, "Free at last! Free at last! Thank God Almighty, we are free at last!"

In his final book, Martin Luther King Jr. asked a pivotal question with the book title, *Where Do We Go from Here: Chaos or Community?*

I can't claim to know what the future holds, but I do know, based on what I've learned writing this book, that we still have a long way to go before all our citizens can equally "thank God Almighty" that "we are free at last!"[112]

While acknowledging the work that needs to be done, we should build on the progress that we have made. Our nation's first African American president offered this insight:

> If you think nothing's changed in the past 50 years, ask somebody who lived through the Selma or Chicago or Los Angeles of the 1950s…To deny this progress—our progress—would be to rob us of our own agency…our responsibility to do what we can to make America better. We know the march is not yet over. We know the race is not yet won. We know that reaching that blessed destination where

we are judged, all of us, by the content of our character requires admitting as much, facing up to the truth…What greater form of patriotism is there than the belief that America is not yet finished, that we are strong enough to be self-critical, that each successive generation can look upon our imperfections and decide that it is in our power to remake this nation to more closely align with our highest ideals? America is a constant work in progress; who believed that loving this country requires more than singing its praises or avoiding uncomfortable truths. It requires the occasional disruption, the willingness to speak out for what is right, to shake up the status quo.[113]

When asked about future generations in general and my grandchildren specifically, my son-in-law said, "In the future there will be these issues, but our child, based on our views, will be armed with knowledge and the correct way to approach these kinds of things. We're not going to pretend it [racism] doesn't exist. We're not going to sugarcoat things, but we're also not going to let it discourage them from doing things they want to do. It [being multiracial] is not a disability or anything that should hold you back. You're a human being on this planet just like anyone else, and you have the same rights as someone else does."[114]

His wife, my daughter, added, "Just like Dr. King, I hope the next generation will be better than ours, and eventually, it will continue to progress."[115]

Pretty good advice from two young people who represent the next generation of leaders who will influence the path our nation takes in the future.

I pray that reading this book encouraged you as much as it did me in writing it. I hope that by learning more about this subject we can shake up the status quo so that when someone grades Dr. King's dreams in the future, we'll be able to acknowledge even more progress—first in ourselves and then in others. Perhaps we can all agree to help others, especially those in need. Perhaps we can reach out to someone who has a different life story and worldview, someone who may look different, or someone who acts or thinks differently because of his or her experiences. In doing this, we may learn a bit about others, and we may learn even more about ourselves.

Please feel free to share your ideas by posting a comment at www.IHaveADreamReportCard.com.

Appendix A

"I Have a Dream" Speech

Speech Available from the US National Archives
(https://www.archives.gov/files/press/exhibits/dream-speech.pdf)

"I HAVE A DREAM . . ."

(Copyright 1963, MARTIN LUTHER KING, JR.)

Speech by the Rev. MARTIN LUTHER KING
At the "March on Washington"

I am happy to join with you today in what will go down in history as the greatest demonstration for freedom in the history of our nation.

Five score years ago, a great American, in whose symbolic shadow we stand today, signed the Emancipation Proclamation. This momentous decree came as a great beacon light of hope to millions of Negro slaves who had been seared in the flames of withering injustice. It came as a joyous daybreak to end the long night of their captivity.

But one hundred years later, the Negro still is not free. One hundred years later, the life of the Negro is still badly crippled by the manacles of segregation and the chains of discrimination. One hundred years later, the Negro lives on a lonely island of poverty in the midst of a vast ocean of material prosperity. One hundred years later, the Negro is still languishing in the corners of American society and finds himself an exile in his own land. So we've come here today to dramatize a shameful condition.

In a sense we have come to our nation's capital to cash a check. When the architects of our Republic wrote the magnificent words of the Constitution and the Declaration of Independence, they were signing a promissory note to which every American was to fall heir. This note was a promise that all men - yes, black men as well as white men - would be guaranteed the unalienable rights of life, liberty, and the pursuit of happiness.

It is obvious today that America has defaulted on this promissory note insofar as her citizens of color are concerned. Instead of honoring this sacred obligation, America has given the Negro people a bad check, a check which has come back marked "insufficient funds."

But we refuse to believe that the bank of justice is bankrupt. We refuse to believe that there are insufficient funds in the great vaults of opportunity of this nation. So we have come to cash this check, a check that will give us upon demand the riches of freedom and the security of justice.

We have also come to this hallowed spot to remind America of the fierce urgency of now. This is no time to engage in the luxury of cooling off or to take the tranquilizing drug of gradualism. Now is the time to make real the promises of democracy. Now is the time to rise from the dark and desolate valley of segregation to the sunlit path of racial justice. Now is the time to lift our nation from the quicksands of racial injustice to the solid rock of brotherhood.

Now is the time to make justice a reality for all of God's children. It would be fatal for the nation to overlook the urgency of the moment. This sweltering summer of the Negro's legitimate discontent will not pass until there is an invigorating autumn of freedom and equality - 1963 is not an end, but a beginning. Those who hope that the Negro needed to blow off steam and will now be content will have a rude awakening if the nation returns to business as usual.

There will be neither rest nor tranquility in America until the Negro is granted his citizenship rights. The whirlwinds of revolt will continue to shake the foundations of our nation until the bright day of justice emerges.

But that is something that I must say to my people who stand on the worn threshold which leads into the palace of justice. In the process of gaining our rightful place we must not be guilty of wrongful deeds. Let us not seek to satisfy our thirst for freedom by drinking from the cup of bitterness and hatred.

We must forever conduct our struggle on the high plane of dignity and discipline. We must not allow our creative protest to degenerate into physical violence. Again and again we must rise to the majestic heights of meeting physical force with soul force. The marvelous new militancy which has engulfed the Negro community must not lead us to distrust all white people, for many of our white brothers, as evidenced by their presence here today, have come to realize that their destiny is tied up with our destiny.

They have come to realize that their freedom is inextricably bound to our freedom. We cannot walk alone. And as we walk, we must make the pledge that we shall always march ahead. We cannot turn back. There are those who are asking the devotees of civil rights, "When will you be satisfied?" We can never be satisfied as long as the Negro is the victim of the unspeakable horrors of police brutality.

We can never be satisfied as long as our bodies, heavy with the fatigue of travel, cannot gain lodging in the motels of the highways and the hotels of the cities.

We cannot be satisfied as long as the Negro's basic mobility is from a smaller ghetto to a larger one. We can never be satisfied as long as our children are stripped of their selfhood and robbed of their dignity by signs stating "For Whites Only."

We cannot be satisfied as long as a Negro in Mississippi cannot vote and a Negro in New York believes he has nothing for which to vote.

No, no, we are not satisfied, and we will not be satisfied until justice rolls down like waters and righteousness like a mighty stream.

I am not unmindful that some of you have come here out of great trials and tribulation. Some of you have come fresh from narrow jail cells. Some of you have come from areas where your quest for freedom left you battered by the storms of persecution and staggered by the winds of police brutality. You have been the veterans of creative suffering.

Continue to work with the faith that unearned suffering is redemptive. Go back to Mississippi, go back to Alabama, go back to South Carolina, go back to Georgia, go back to Louisiana, go back to the slums and ghettos of our northern cities, knowing that somehow this situation can and will be changed. Let us not wallow in the valley of despair.

I say to you today, my friends, so even though we face the difficulties of today and tomorrow, I still have a dream. It is a dream deeply rooted in the American dream. I have a dream that one day this nation will rise up, live out the true meaning of its creed: "We hold these truths to be self-evident: that all men are created equal."

I have a dream that one day on the red hills of Georgia the sons of former slaves and the sons of former slave-owners will be able to sit down together at the table of brotherhood.

I have a dream that one day even the state of Mississippi, a state sweltering with the heat of injustice, sweltering with the heat of oppression, will be transformed into an oasis of freedom and justice.

I have a dream that my four little children will one day live in a nation where they will not be judged by the color of their skin but by the content of their character. I have a dream today ... I have a dream that one day in Alabama, with its vicious racists, with its governor having his lips dripping with the words of interposition and nullification; one day right there in Alabama, little black boys and black girls will be able to join hands with little white boys and white girls as sisters and brothers.

I have a dream today ... I have a dream that one day every valley shall be exalted, every hill and mountain shall be made low. The rough places will be made plain, and the crooked places will be made straight, and the glory of the Lord shall be revealed, and all flesh shall see it together. This is our hope. This is the faith that I go back to the South with. With this faith we will be able to hew out of the mountain of despair a stone of hope. With this faith we will be able to transform the jangling discords of our nation into a beautiful symphony of brotherhood. With this faith we will be able to work together, to pray together, to struggle together, to go to jail together, to stand up for freedom together, knowing that we will be free one day.

This will be the day when all of God's children will be able to sing with a new meaning. "My country, 'tis of thee, sweet land of liberty, of thee I sing. Land where my fathers died, land of the pilgrim's pride, from every mountainside, let freedom ring." And if America is to be a great nation this must become true. So let freedom ring from the prodigious hilltops of New Hampshire. Let freedom ring from the mighty mountains of New York. Let freedom ring from the heightening Alleghenies of Pennsylvania! Let freedom ring from the snowcapped Rockies of Colorado! Let freedom ring from the curvaceous slopes of California!

But not only that; let freedom ring from Stone Mountain of Georgia! Let freedom ring from Lookout Mountain of Tennessee! Let freedom ring from every hill and molehill of Mississippi, from every mountainside. Let freedom ring.

When we allow freedom to ring - when we let it ring from every city and every hamlet, from every state and every city, we will be able to speed up that day when all of God's children, black men and white men, Jews and Gentiles, Protestants and Catholics, will be able to join hands and sing in the words of the old Negro spiritual, "Free at last, Free at last, Great God Almighty, We are free at last."

Appendix B

Interview Guide

How did you feel the first time you heard Dr. King's "I Have a Dream" speech? Note: If you can't remember hearing Dr. King's speech, or it's been a while since you heard it, invest fifteen minutes and listen to it here: https://www.youtube.com/watch?v=H0yP4aLyq1g

What inspired you about Dr. King's work for civil rights?

Do you remember how you felt when you first learned that Dr. King had been assassinated; or how did you feel the first time you studied about the death of Dr. King as part of our American history?

I'm going to share a grading scale with you and would like for you to grade the following "dreams" based on this scale. Please briefly describe why you offered your grade.

> A = true today
> B = mostly true today
> C = significant progress made, but work still
>   remains
> D = lack of sufficient progress made
> F = little to no progress made

I have a dream that my four little children will one day live in a nation where they will not be judged by the color of their skin but by the content of their character.

I have a dream that one day…the sons of former slaves and the sons of former slave owners will be able to sit down together at the table of brotherhood.

I have a dream that one day…little black boys and black girls will be able to join hands with little white boys and white girls as sisters and brothers.

Now is the time to make real the promises of democracy.

Now is the time to rise from the dark and desolate valley of segregation to the sunlit path of racial justice. Now is the time to lift our nation from the quicksands of racial injustice to the solid rock of brotherhood. Now is the time to make justice a reality for all of God's children.

We cannot be satisfied as long as a Negro in Mississippi cannot vote and a Negro in New York believes he has nothing for which to vote.

We can never be satisfied, as long as our bodies, heavy with the fatigue of travel, cannot gain lodging in the motels of the highways and the hotels of the cities.

We can never be satisfied as long as our children are stripped of their selfhood and robbed of their dignity by signs stating "For Whites Only."

We can never be satisfied as long as the Negro is the victim of the unspeakable horrors of police brutality.

We cannot be satisfied as long as the Negro's basic mobility is from a smaller ghetto to a larger one.

In the process of gaining our rightful place we must not be guilty of wrongful deeds. Let us not seek to satisfy our thirst for freedom by drinking from the cup of bitterness and hatred. We must forever conduct our struggle on the high plane of dignity and discipline. We must not allow our creative protest to degenerate into physical violence.

Do you have any personal experiences or anecdotes you'd like to share about the continuing struggle for civil rights?

During Dr. King's "I Have a Dream" speech, he said, "There are those who are asking the devotees of civil rights, 'When will you be satisfied?'" If someone asked you, "When will you be satisfied?," how would you respond?

Do you know of others who would be interested in participating in this project? If so, please provide their name, title, and contact information.

Acknowledgments

First, I want to acknowledge the great sacrifice made by Dr. Martin Luther King Jr. and his family. He was assassinated three months before I was born, so I have no firsthand accounts of what he or his family went through during their struggle for equal rights. I only know what can be gleaned from a historical perspective. What I do know is that the dream he offered from the steps of the Lincoln Memorial on August 28, 1963, has not been achieved.

I also know that the work continues through organizations such as the Martin Luther King Jr. Center for Nonviolent Social Change (a.k.a. the King Center) in Atlanta, Georgia. Dr. King's widow, Coretta Scott King, established the center in 1968, the same year of Dr. King's death, to serve as a "living memorial filled with all the vitality that was his, a center of human endeavor, committed to the causes for which he lived and died."[116] More information is available at www.thekingcenter.org.

Another great organization continuing the work of Dr. King is the National Civil Rights Museum, located in my current hometown of Memphis, Tennessee. The museum offers a full immersion experience providing visitors with the ability to "learn about historical milestones [and] interpret them in a way that can be applied to today's challenges."[117] I feel so strongly about their work that all proceeds from the sale of this book are being donated to the museum. Those interested in supporting this museum can visit www.civilrightsmuseum.org.

I appreciate the insights offered by Jim Wallis, Sojourners president and founder and best-selling author of *America's Original Sin: Racism, White Privilege, and the Bridge to a New America*. I doubt I could have finished this project without the great research presented by Mr. Wallis. I quoted extensively from his book (with proper citations, of course) and used many of the same sources for my secondary research. Headquartered in Washington, DC, the folks at Sojourners make a positive impact through their mission of articulating "the biblical call to social justice, to inspire hope and build a movement to transform individuals, communities, the church, and the world."[118] I encourage those with a passion for social justice to support their work and subscribe to their magazine at www.sojo.net.

About the Author

Alvin Plexico, Ph.D.
Commander, U.S. Navy (Retired)

As a lifelong learner, Dr. Plexico enjoys teaching graduate and undergraduate courses in communication, crisis management, ethics, leadership, management, organizational behavior, organizational development and change, public speaking, qualitative research, social media, and strategy.

A 22-year Navy career included service as a Pentagon Press Officer, a Spokesperson for the U.S. Pacific Fleet, and Director of Communication of the Center for Career Development.

He earned a Bachelor's Degree in Business Management, a Master's Degree in Communication, and a Doctor of Philosophy in Organizational Leadership.

Alvin and his wife of 30 years, Lucinda, currently live near Memphis, Tennessee. Their youngest daughter, Savannah, serves others as a social worker and their oldest daughter, Shiloh, serves in the Air Force.

Alvin enjoys reading, running, and following Texas Rangers baseball. He's creatively found ways to do two of these at the same time, but has yet to discover a way to do all three. In an attempt to diversify his physical activities, he races in triathlons, with the ultimate goal of completing an Ironman.

Dr. Plexico enjoys connecting with other lifelong learners through his blog at www.drplexico.com .

Notes

---

1 Memphis Dream Center, http://memphisdreamcenter.com/about-mdc.

2 Martin Luther King Jr., "Remaining Awake through a Great Revolution," commencement address at Oberlin College, June 1965, http://www.oberlin.edu/external/EOG/BlackHistoryMonth/MLK/CommAddress.html.

3 Nicholas Kristof, "When Whites Just Don't Get It, Part 3," *New York Times*, October 11, 2014, http://www.nytimes.com/2014/10/12/opinion/sunday/nicholas-kristof-when-whites-just-dont-get-it-part-3.html?_r=0.

4 Keenan Stovall, interview, Augusta, Georgia, July 29, 2017.

5 Ibid.

6 Ibid.

7 Jim Wallis, *America's Original Sin: Racism, White Privilege, and the Bridge to a New America* (Grand Rapids, MI: Brazos, 2016).

8 Ibid.

9 Cheryl Staats, "State of the Science: Implicit Bias Review 2014," Kirwan Institute for the Study of Race and Ethnicity, Ohio State University, March 2014, http://kirwaninstitute.osu.edu/wp-content/uploads/2014/03/2014-implicit-bias.pdf, 72.

10 Robert P. Jones, "Self-Segregation: Why It's So Hard for Whites to Understand Ferguson," *Atlantic Monthly*, August 21, 2014, http://www.theatlantic.com/national/archive/2014/08/self-segregation-why-its-hard-for-whites-to-understand-ferguson/378928/, cited in Jim Wallis, *America's Original Sin:*

Racism, White Privilege, and the Bridge to a New America (Grand Rapids, MI: Brazos, 2016).

[11] Jim Wallis, *America's Original Sin: Racism, White Privilege, and the Bridge to a New America* (Grand Rapids, MI: Brazos, 2016).

[12] Robert Jensen, "How White Privilege Shapes the US," *Beyond Whiteness*, http://www.beyondwhiteness.com/2012/02/23/robert-jensen-how-white-privilege-shapes-the-u-s/#sthash.XXCrRk7y.dpuf.

[13] Paul Alexander, "Raced as White," *PRISM*, July 1, 2013, http://prismmagazine.org/raced-as-white/.

[14] Pew Research Center Population Projections, http://www.pewresearch.org/topics/population-projections/.

[15] Martin Luther King Jr., "I Have a Dream" speech, Lincoln Memorial, Washington, DC, August 28, 1963.

[16] Jim Wallis, *America's Original Sin: Racism, White Privilege, and the Bridge to a New America* (Grand Rapids, MI: Brazos, 2016).

[17] Ibid.

[18] Sophia Kerby, "The Top 10 Most Startling Facts about People of Color and Criminal Justice in the United States," Center for American Progress, March 13, 2012, https://www.americanprogress.org/issues/race/news/2012/03/13/11351/the-top-10-most-startling-facts-about-people-of-color-and-criminal-justice-in-the-united-states/.

[19] Leah Sakala, "Breaking Down Mass Incarceration in the 2010 Census: State-by-State Incarceration Rates by Race/Ethnicity," Prison Policy Initiative, May 28, 2014, http://www.prisonpolicy.org/reports/rates.html, cited in Jim Wallis, *America's Original Sin: Racism, White Privilege, and the Bridge to*

a New America (loc. 1542–1544, Kindle).

[20] Kelly Welch, "Black Criminal Stereotypes and Racial Profiling," *Journal of Contemporary Criminal Justice* 23 (2007): 280. doi: 10.1177/1043986207306870.

[21] Ibid.

[22] African Americans are about three times more likely to be arrested than are whites. "Racial Disparities in Arrests Are Prevalent, but Cause Isn't Clear," NPR.org, November 23, 2014, http://www.npr.org/blogs/codeswitch/2014/11/23/366159956/racial-disparities-in-arrests-are-prevalent-but-cause-isnt-clear.

[23] Sophia Kerby, "Top 10 Most Startling Facts," cited in Jim Wallis, *America's Original Sin: Racism, White Privilege, and the Bridge to a New America* (loc. 3630–3631, Kindle).

[24] Ibid.

[25] Bureau of Justice Statistics, "More Than 60% of the People in Prison Today Are People of Color, 'Fact Sheet: Trends in US Corrections'" (Washington, DC: Sentencing Project), updated April 2015, http://sentencingproject.org/doc/publications/inc_Trends_in_Correct ions_Fact_sheet.pdf, 5.

[26] "Fact Sheet: Trends in US Corrections" (Washington, DC: Sentencing Project), updated April 2015, http://sentencingproject.org/doc/publications/inc_Trends_in_Correct ions_Fact_sheet.pdf, 2.

[27] Jim Wallis, *America's Original Sin: Racism, White Privilege, and the Bridge to a New America* (Grand Rapids, MI: Brazos, 2016).

[28] Michelle Alexander, "How to Dismantle the 'New Jim Crow,'"

Sojourners, July 2014, http://sojo.net/magazine/2014/07/how-dismantle-new-jim-crow.

29 President's Task Force, Interim Report, cited in Jim Wallis, *America's Original Sin: Racism, White Privilege, and the Bridge to a New America* (loc. 3186–3191, Kindle).

30 Jim Wallis, *America's Original Sin: Racism, White Privilege, and the Bridge to a New America* (Grand Rapids, MI: Brazos, 2016).

31 "Criminal Justice Facts," Sentencing Project, http://www.sentencingproject.org/criminal-justice-facts/.

32 Martin Luther King Jr., *Stride toward Freedom: The Montgomery Story* (Boston: Beacon, 2010).

33 Jim Wallis, *America's Original Sin: Racism, White Privilege, and the Bridge to a New America* (Grand Rapids, MI: Brazos, 2016).

34 Benjamin Mueller and Al Baker, "2 NYPD Officers Killed in Brooklyn Ambush," *New York Times*, December 20, 2014, https://www.nytimes.com/2014/12/21/nyregion/two-police-officers-shot-in-their-patrol-car-in-brooklyn.html.

35 *Preliminary 2014 Law Enforcement Officer Fatalities Report* (Washington, DC: National Law Enforcement Officers Memorial Fund, 2015), http://www.nleomf.org/assets/pdfs/reports/Preliminary-2014-Officer-Fatalities-Report.pdf, 1.

36 Elizabeth Bristow, "ERLC President Russell Moore Responds to Grand Jury Decision in Ferguson," The Ethics and Religious Liberty Commission of the Southern Baptist Convention, November 24, 2014, http://erlc.com/article/erlc-president-russell-moore-responds-to-grand-jury-decision-in-ferguson.

37 Dara Lind, "FBI Trying to Get Better Data," cited in Jim Wallis,

America's Original Sin: Racism, White Privilege, and the Bridge to a New America (Grand Rapids, MI: Brazos, 2016).

38 Steve Cohen, "FBI Director Is Right, Police Departments Should Have to Report Police Shootings," Office of Rep. Steve Cohen, February 12, 2015, http://cohen.house.gov/press-release/congressman-cohen-fbi-director-right-police-departments-should-have-report-police.

39 Black Lives Matter, http://blacklivesmatter.com/.

40 Shiloh Stovall, interview, Augusta, Georgia, July 29, 2017.

41 Ibid.

42 Adam Johnson, AlterNet, July 23, 2015, http://www.alternet.org/media/5-minutes-larry-wilmore-explains-why-saying-alllivesmatter-offensive.

43 Martin Luther King Jr., "I Have a Dream" speech, Lincoln Memorial, Washington, DC, August 28, 1963.

44 Martin Luther King Jr., "The Quest for Peace and Justice," Nobel lecture, December 11, 1964, http://www.nobelprize.org/nobel_prizes/peace/laureates/1964/king-lecture.html.

45 *Bill of Rights*, The National Archives, https://www.archives.gov/founding-docs/bill-of-rights-transcript.

46 Wendi C. Thomas, "Take It to the Bridge," MLK50 Justice through Journalism, July 7, 2017, https://mlk50.com/july-10-2016-take-it-to-the-bridge-e13744c16c21.

47 NAACP Statement following bridge protest, July 10, 2016, http://wreg.com/2016/07/10/interim-mpd-director-shows-up-to-

black-lives-matter-rally/.

[48] Jim Wallis, *America's Original Sin: Racism, White Privilege, and the Bridge to a New America* (Grand Rapids, MI: Brazos, 2016).

[49] Steve Wyche, National Football League, August 27, 2016, http://www.nfl.com/news/story/0ap3000000691077/article/colin-kaepernick-explains-why-he-sat-during-national-anthem.

[50] Ibid.

[51] Keenan Stovall, interview, Augusta, Georgia, July 29, 2017.

[52] Martin Luther King Jr., "I Have a Dream" speech, Lincoln Memorial, Washington, DC, August 28, 1963.

[53] United States Court of Appeals for the Fourth Circuit, July 29, 2016, http://electionlawblog.org/wp-content/uploads/nc-4th.pdf.

[54] Brennan Center for Justice at New York University School of Law, January 31, 2017, https://www.brennancenter.org/analysis/debunking-voter-fraud-myth.

[55] Brennan Center for Justice at New York University School of Law, November 9, 2007, https://www.brennancenter.org/publication/truth-about-voter-fraud.

[56] Justin Levitt, "A Comprehensive Investigation of Voter Impersonation Finds 31 Credible Incidents Out of One Billion Ballots Cast," *Washington Post*, August 6, 2014, https://www.washingtonpost.com/news/wonk/wp/2014/08/06/a-comprehensive-investigation-of-voter-impersonation-finds-31-credible-incidents-out-of-one-billion-ballots-cast/?utm_term=.654d785d0cdc.

[57] Ibid.

[58] Lorraine C. Minnite, "The Politics of Voter Fraud," Columbia University, March 2007, http://www.projectvote.org/wp-content/uploads/2007/03/Politics_of_Voter_Fraud_Final.pdf

[59] Ibid.

[60] Ibid.

[61] Jim Wallis, *America's Original Sin* (Grand Rapids, MI: Brazos, 2016, loc. 3785, Kindle).

[62] Vanessa M. Perez, "Americans with Photo ID: A Breakdown of Demographic Characteristics," Project Vote research memo, February 2015, http://www.projectvote.org/wp-content/uploads/2015/06/AMERICANS-WITH-PHOTO-ID-Research-Memo-February-2015.pdf.

[63] Nicole Tuner-Lee, "Trump's Election Integrity Commission Needs to Redress Voter Suppression, Not Voter Fraud," Brookings Institution, June 21, 2017, https://www.brookings.edu/blog/fixgov/2017/06/21/voter-suppression-and-election-integrity-commission/?utm_campaign=Brookings%20Brief&utm_source=hs_email&utm_medium=email&utm_content=54004924.

[64] Brennan Center for Justice at New York University School of Law, "Citizens without Proof: A Survey of Americans' Possession of Documentary Proof of Citizenship and Photo Identification," November 2006, http://www.brennancenter.org/sites/default/files/legacy/d/download_file_39242.pdf.

[65] Christopher Ingraham, "This Is the Best Explanation of Gerrymandering You Will Ever See," *Washington Post*, March 1,

2015,
https://www.washingtonpost.com/news/wonk/wp/2015/03/01/this-is-the-best-explanation-of-gerrymandering-you-will-ever-see/?utm_term=.38396f0d8e90.

[66] *Thornburg v. Gingles*, December 4, 1985,
https://www.oyez.org/cases/1985/83-1968?page=10.

[67] Adam Liptak, "Supreme Court Invalidates Key Part of Voting Rights Act," *New York Times*, June 25, 2013,
http://www.nytimes.com/2013/06/26/us/supreme-court-ruling.html.

[68] Ibid.

[69] Ibid.

[70] Ibid.

[71] Drew Desilver, "5 Facts about Economic Inequality," Pew Research Center, January 7, 2014, http://www.pewresearch.org/fact-tank/2014/01/07/5-facts-about-economic-inequality/.

[72] Rakesh Kochhar and Richard Fry, "Wealth Inequality Has Widened along Racial, Ethnic Lines since End of Great Recession," Pew Research Center, December 12, 2014,
http://www.pewresearch.org/fact-tank/2014/12/12/racial-wealth-gaps-great-recession/.

[73] Ibid.

[74] Suzanne Macartney, Alemayehu Bishaw, and Kayla Fontenot, "Poverty Rates for Selected Detailed Race and Hispanic Groups by State and Place: 2007–2011," US Census Bureau, February 2013,
https://www.census.gov/prod/2013pubs/acsbr11-17.pdf.

[75] Ibid.

76 "The Unemployment Situation," White House Archives, February 5, 2016, https://obamawhitehouse.archives.gov/blog/2016/02/05/employment-situation-january.

77 "Two Putting the Economy and Jobs in Perspective," Carolina Small Business Development Fund, September 9, 2013, https://carolinasmallbusiness.org/2013/09/two-charts-putting-the-economy-and-jobs-in-perspective/.

78 Martin Luther King Jr., "I Have a Dream" speech, Lincoln Memorial, Washington, DC, August 28, 1963.
79 Ibid.

80 "Equal Access to Accommodations," Virginia Historical Society, http://www.vahistorical.org/collections-and-resources/virginia-history-explorer/civil-rights-movement-virginia/equal-access.

81 Maria Goodavage, "'Green Book' Helped Keep African Americans Safe on the Road," PBS, January 10, 2013, http://www.pbs.org/independentlens/blog/green-book-helped-keep-african-americans-safe-on-the-road/.

82 Ibid.

83 Ibid.

84 Ibid.

85 Ibid.

86 "Civil Rights Act of 1964," National Archives, https://www.ourdocuments.gov/doc.php?flash=false&doc=97.

87 "Martin Luther King, Jr. Questioned Issues of Faith, New Volume Reveals," *King Encyclopedia*, Stanford University, http://mlk-kpp01.stanford.edu/kingweb/news/vol6announcement.htm.

88 Michael O. Emerson, "A New Day for Multiracial Congregations," *Reflections*, Yale University, spring 2013, http://reflections.yale.edu/article/future-race/new-day-multiracial-congregations, cited in Jim Wallis, *America's Original Sin: Racism, White Privilege, and the Bridge to a New America* (Kindle).

89 Jim Wallis, *America's Original Sin: Racism, White Privilege, and the Bridge to a New America* (Grand Rapids, MI: Brazos, 2016, loc. 2919–2923, Kindle).

90 Martin Luther King Jr., "Letter from a Birmingham Jail," African Studies Center, University of Pennsylvania, April 16, 1963, http://www.africa.upenn.edu/Articles_Gen/Letter_Birmingham.html.

91 John Sides, "White Christian America Is Dying," *Washington Post*, August 15, 2016, https://www.washingtonpost.com/news/monkey-cage/wp/2016/08/15/white-christian-america-is-dying/?utm_term=.cbb210064c00.

92 Ibid.

93 Ibid.

94 Ibid.

95 The Life Church, http://thelifechurch.com/pages/vision-values.

96 Johnny Hill, interview, Memphis, Tennessee, July 18, 2017.

97 Ibid.

[98] Ibid.

[99] "2010 Faith Communities Today Survey,"
http://faithcommunitiestoday.org/sites/default/files/2010Frequencies
V1.pdf.

[100] Michael O. Emerson, "A New Day for Multiracial
Congregations," *Reflections*, Yale University, spring 2013,
http://reflections.yale.edu/article/future-race/new-day-multiracial-
congregations.

[101] Ibid.

[102] Ibid.

[103] Bob Smietana, "Churches Open Doors to All," *USA Today*,
September 18, 2012,
http://usatoday30.usatoday.com/news/nation/story/2012/09/18/churc
hes-open-doors-to-all/57798200/1, cited in Jim Wallis, *America's
Original Sin: Racism, White Privilege, and the Bridge to a New
America* (Kindle).

[104] Martin Luther King Jr., "I Have a Dream" speech, Lincoln
Memorial, Washington, DC, August 28, 1963.

[105] Gretchen Livingston and Anna Brown, "Intermarriage in the US
50 Years after *Loving v. Virginia*," Pew Research Center, May 18,
2017, http://www.pewsocialtrends.org/2017/05/18/intermarriage-in-
the-u-s-50-years-after-loving-v-virginia/.

[106] Ibid.

[107] Hansi Lo Wang, National Public Radio, May 18, 2017, based on
Pew Research Center Report,
http://www.npr.org/sections/codeswitch/2017/05/18/528939766/five
-fold-increase-in-interracial-marriages-50-years-after-they-became-

legal.

108 Johnny Hill, interview, Memphis, Tennessee, July 28, 2017.

109 Coretta Scott King, speech at Lambda Legal, Chicago, March 31, 1998, quoted in Reuters.

110 Coretta Scott King, *Chicago Tribune*, April 1, 1998.

111 John Blake, CNN, January 16, 2012, http://religion.blogs.cnn.com/2012/01/16/what-did-mlk-think-about-gay-people/.

112 Martin Luther King Jr., "I Have a Dream" speech, Lincoln Memorial, Washington, DC, August 28, 1963.

113 Barack Obama, "Remarks by the President at the 50th Anniversary of the Selma to Montgomery Marches," White House Office of the Press Secretary, March 7, 2015, https://www.whitehouse.gov/the-press-office/2015/03/07/remarks-president-50th-anniversary-selma-montgomery-marches, cited in Jim Wallis, *America's Original Sin: Racism, White Privilege, and the Bridge to a New America* (Kindle).

114 Keenan Stovall, interview, Augusta, Georgia, July 29, 2017.

115 Shiloh Stovall, interview, Augusta, Georgia, July 29, 2017.

116 King Center, http://www.thekingcenter.org/about-king-center.

117 National Civil Rights Museum, http://www.civilrightsmuseum.org/learn.

118 Sojourners, https://sojo.net/about-us/who-we-are.

www.ingramcontent.com/pod-product-compliance
Lightning Source LLC
Chambersburg PA
CBHW070815240726
48654CB00007B/357